# MIND
# YOUR
# MUSIC

# MIND YOUR MUSIC

## JOHN HENRY SHERIDAN

Brooklyn, New York

Mind Your Music
© 2021 Paperback. John Henry Sheridan.

All rights reserved.
Please share thoughtfully and considerately.

For specific permission requests, write to the publisher,
addressed "Attention: Permissions Coordinator,"
at the address below.

johnhenrysheridan@gmail.com

Mind Your Music / John Henry Sheridan
ISBN: 979-8-9852523-0-9
Published by Coral Sound Publishing

Editing by Sacred Dragon Publishing
Front Cover and Illustration by Francine Marie Sheppard
Back Cover and Book Layout by Ryan Forsythe

*Disclaimer: John Henry Sheridan is not a doctor nor a physical specialist of any sort. Please examine the ideas he presents in this book with a critical lens as to how and if they apply to your life. Please approach any physical recommendations with caution. The author shall not be held responsible for misuse of the material. The purpose of this book is to inspire, educate and entertain.*

# DEDICATION

This book is dedicated to all Music Lovers.

~ ~ ~

"In one of his writings Nichiren Daishonin cites the words, 'We can discern a country's rise and fall by whether its tones are happy or sad'. Namely, the sounds prevailing in a society at any given time can help us understand a country's future, whether it is destined to flourish or decline. These sounds are the sounds of human voices and, by extension, of culture and the arts, including, of course, music."

- Daisaku Ikeda (Buddhist philosopher and leader)

~ ~ ~

"If one should desire to know whether a kingdom is well governed, if its morals are good or bad, the quality of its music is going to furnish the answer."

- Confucius (renowned Chinese philosopher)

~ ~ ~

"Music is the universal language, sound can prevent and heal you from disease. High vibration music is key in these times."

- *Feel Alive* by Ralph Smart (Infinite Waters)

# ACKNOWLEDGEMENTS

<u>Huge THANK YOU:</u>

To all my favorite bands and players who inspired me to want to pick up the guitar in the first place.

To all the music teachers, fellow musicians, and students who have enriched and colored my life.

To all the many friends and fans who have supported my musical path in one way or another throughout the years.

To the many independent authors who came before me showing by example how it can be done, especially Bob Baker.

To all the many amazing human beings who operate within the sphere of the music and Health relationship.

<u>Personal THANK YOU:</u>

To my mother Linda for endless support, encouragement, and acceptance of my chosen musical life path.

To my wife Yoko for love, patience, support, and for directly assisting me to bring this book into reality.

To Andi and Sacred Dragon Publishing for enormous support, guidance, and encouragement without which this book would not be what it has become.

To Jason Hills for invaluable support of my musical career throughout many years of friendship and teamwork.

To Daisaku Ikeda, my mentor in life, for showing me by example the vast potential that exists in my own life.

# TABLE OF CONTENTS

|  |  |  |
|---|---|---|
|  | PREFACE | ix |
| Chapter 1 | BEAUTIFUL MUSIC AND VIBRANT HEALTH ARE HARMONIOUS | 1 |
| Chapter 2 | WHY IS THE *MIND YOUR MUSIC* CONVERSATION RELEVANT? | 11 |
| Chapter 3 | MUSIC CAN ENRICH OUR LIVES | 23 |
| Chapter 4 | THE SLIDING SCALE OF UNHEALTHY TO HEALTHY MUSIC | 35 |
| Chapter 5 | HOW CAN YOU FIND THE BEST MUSIC FOR YOU? | 51 |
| Chapter 6 | MUSIC AS MAGIC | 63 |
|  | CONCLUSION | 75 |
| Appendix A | TEN WAYS TO ENRICH YOUR LIFE WITH MUSIC | 79 |
| Appendix B | JOHN HENRY'S RECOMMENDED LISTENING LIST | 93 |
| Appendix C | ADDITIONAL RESOURCES | 104 |
|  | ABOUT THE AUTHOR | 111 |

# PREFACE

Originally, this book *Mind Your Music* began as a 2nd edition of my 2016 e-book *Music for Health: How Understanding the Power of Music Can Improve the Quality of Your Life*. After wrestling with the content of the original book for some time, I recognized that the message I truly wanted to convey would be more clearly achieved through the framework of a different book title with a bit of a different approach, flavor, and reworking. Perhaps my main stumbling block was how I used the word *health* in the e-book *Music for Health*. I have since become more acutely aware that the word *health* can have certain limiting associations (such as being limited to the physical body, exercise, and diet, as well as the medical and health care industries). While I am not excluding those fields, I am speaking to a much larger picture.

I wish there were a term that encapsulates all that I am pointing to with the word health. But since I do not know of one, I will use the word Health with an uppercase H throughout this book. So, for the purposes of this book, when I use the term Health, I intend it in its most expansive definition to include all aspects of Health: physical, mental, emotional, environmental, social, and spiritual. I am also broadly implying what can be understood as "well-being" when I use the term Health in the context of this writing. As you read, I invite you to think of Health in its broadest possible sense as if it encompasses everything that makes life enjoyable and worth living.

## The Purpose of This Book

My intentions in writing this book can be summed up in 4 main points:

1. Raise awareness about the profound connection between music and Health,
2. Highlight the profusion of benefits and potentials for enrichment that music can provide while acknowledging its significant potential for harm,
3. Instill a sense of empowerment and excitement around choosing the best music to enrich and enhance your life,
4. Offer some practical ways you can apply this insight into enriching your life through music beginning now.

## Allow Me to Introduce Myself

Hi, my name is John Henry Sheridan. I believe in the power of music and always have as far back as I can remember. Having spent so much time in my younger years pursuing the rock star dream (among other musical dreams), I have grown to think more deeply about how the influences in my own life, particularly musical, have affected me in both positive and negative ways.

I have experienced firsthand various detrimental effects that both the music and my lifestyle as a musician in previous times have had on my Health. Those experiences inspired me to deeply explore my relationship with music and make a conscious choice to use it to enrich, rather than diminish, my life. I am sharing what I have learned from deeply living with music throughout my life in the hopes of empowering you to have the most positive relationship with music possible.

For example, I have experienced firsthand the benefit of cleansing my music library of the artists, albums, and songs that I had noticed over time were detracting from my quality of life. When I eliminated the albums that I found to be more destructive and divisive (rather than positive and unifying), I noticed that my life started to feel lighter, happier, freer, and overall Healthier.

This isn't to say that I then excluded all these artists and albums from my life completely. Not at all. I still enjoy listening to some of the rock and heavy metal music of my past, but I no longer have much of it in my possession, tempting me to listen to it all the time. Knowing that some of the music I like to listen to may not have been created from a kind-hearted place, I no longer want the potentially negative energies of its creation continually vying for my attention by being present on a shelf in my home or in my digital music library.

Cleansing my music library of negative energy truly helped me free up some of my own energy for moving my life in a more positive direction. My sensitivity to energy has also made me very conscientious about the lyrics that I write and the life condition and moods that I intentionally imbue into my own compositions. I have also become conscious of the overall trajectory of my musical path upon the human spirit and aspire to be contributive in the highest sense that I am capable of.

By undergoing this process, I have personally witnessed how we are all sensitive to the energetic influences of music, whether we realize it or not. We can either be brought down by or raised up by it. With that insight in mind, I want to share the following point, which I truly believe:

*A right relationship to music can truly benefit any human being and society as a whole.*

From my experience, I know this to be true. I have written this book *Mind Your Music* to share my thoughts, philosophy, and personal experiences regarding the link between music and our Health. I regard this writing as a philosophy book and a self-help teaching memoir. I am not claiming it to be a scholarly work, but rather a heart-based offering that seeks to tap the vast resources of my life experiences to help empower us humans to live

# Preface

the most expansive, joyful, and fulfilling life possible by speaking to and clarifying our profound relationship to music.

Throughout the book, I am primarily speaking from my own experience and perspective. While I do incorporate various bits of information that I learned from some basic research that I did for the writing of this book, I do not include detailed references or cite specific science to prove my points. For those of you who would like to dive deeper into the subject, however, I have included an "Additional Resources" section at the end of the book where you can find plenty of information for learning more about the valuable connection between music and Health.

If you would like to discover more deeply all the science and research being done in connection to the profound power of, and connection between, music and Health, please do a quick search of the topic on the internet. You could try some simple questions like "Can music affect my health and well-being?" or "What is the relationship between health, well-being, and music?" You could also try searching something like "music benefits" or conversely "unhealthy music" or "Can music be unhealthy?". You may be surprised at just how much information pops up around the profound impact (both positive and negative) music can and does indeed have on our precious lives.

I understand that my unscientific and less-than-scholarly approach may not appeal to everyone. If,

Mind Your Music

however, you are interested in learning from the insight and practical wisdom wrought from many years of musical experience, life experience, and strong conviction in the value of leading a happy, joyful, and contributive life, then please read on. I assure you, consideration of the ideas that I offer within these pages at the very least will do you no harm, and in their highest potential, will uplift and inspire you in very real ways.

# CHAPTER 1

# BEAUTIFUL MUSIC AND VIBRANT HEALTH ARE HARMONIOUS

This is a book about the profound relationship between music and our Health.[1] So, let's start with the basics and address some fundamental philosophical questions that perhaps you have not consciously thought about. I'd like to invite you to ponder these questions with an expansive mind, as both a spiritual and physical being, if you will, as I extrapolate and share my thoughts with you.

## What is Music?

You could look it up in the dictionary and get some technical ideas about melody, pitch, intervals, rhythm, and other information about the elements and components of music – all of which describe music by its *features*. One of the ways Merriam-Webster Dictionary defines *music* is "The science or art of ordering tones or

---

[1] As I mentioned in the "Preface," for the purposes of this book I will use the term Health with an uppercase H implying Health in its broadest possible sense to include all aspects of Health: physical, mental, emotional, environmental, social, and spiritual. I am also encompassing what is generally understood as "well-being" when I use the term Health.

sounds in succession, in combination, and in temporal relationships to produce a composition having unity and continuity." No doubt there may be some value in understanding the features of music as described above.

I do wonder though, to what extent is there a common consensus among all humans as to just what exactly music is? For example, would you consider a series of intermittent horns honking in rush hour traffic to be music? I imagine most would not (perhaps some would). Would you consider a baby crying to be music? Probably not, but perhaps a little. What about a birdsong? Ahh . . .well, now we must pause. This does indeed contain several of the elements of music, such as melody, pitch, and rhythm, and after all, it is referred to as a "song," which is a musical term. But you are not likely to find the lovely birdsong of a nightingale on the Billboard Top 100 list, are you?

When I ask myself on the deepest level, "What is music?" I get a different answer than most classic textbook definitions might offer. For me, at its most *essential* level, music is simply a form of communication and expression. Both communication and expression are fundamental aspects of being human and thus perhaps why music is so intrinsically connected to who we are.

There are many examples of music as communication and expression. A parent sings or hums to their infant to let them know that they are nearby and all is well.

In the plantation fields of early American history, slaves sang phrases back and forth to one another to keep one another's spirits up, express their emotions, and pass the time. This call-and-answer style "field holler," as it is known, is an essential part of the history of how blues music later developed in the early 20th century. Blues music itself is a great example of communicating and expressing one's basic feelings within a familiar form that is potentially accessible to anyone. Further, individuals within groups of tribal hunters on the plains of Africa, for example, would use musical vocalizing and drumming to communicate with each other from far distances. The battle cries and horn-blowing of medieval and ancient Europeans were intended to fiercely rouse courage and frighten the enemy while communicating the extreme importance of everyone putting their all into the battle at hand.

One of the key ways that music communicates and expresses is as a form of exultation, or you could say worship and communion with the divine - that which is greater than our individual small selves. Classical music of both India and China was very highly regarded and even revered. These musical forms communicated and expressed to the listener the divine nature of creation, and music of this sort was essentially thought of as serving and worshipping the gods. Similarly, classical music of Europe was primarily divinely informed and inspired. Many composers, such as renowned classical composer J.S. Bach, for example, composed numerous masterpieces within and with the support of the church for the greater glory of God.

When we bear in mind this *essential* definition of music, as communication, expression, and further exultation, it can serve to unite us on a deep level with ourselves, with society, and with the world at large. From this perspective, the impact of music emanating from a pure-hearted source can be profound. However, when we only define music by its *features* rather than its *essence*, we may come to commodify it and exploit it for personal gain to the exclusion of others.

When we glance at the history of music, we see that it wasn't until fairly recent times that musicians could become celebrities capable of attracting and accumulating an imbalanced sense of power, influence, and material riches. Historically speaking, the purpose of music for many centuries and perhaps millennia was truly service-oriented and aimed at honoring something greater than oneself while unifying and bringing joy and harmony to both self and others.

I would suggest that the reckless lives that we see being lived by many musical celebrities in this modern era have gone far astray from the original essential role that music played in the heart of humanity. When we look at music within a historical context of hundreds or even thousands of years, we can sense that somewhere in the not-too-distant past, music had a purity that has since been obscured and sometimes completely lost in our materialistic consumer culture. We have inherited a culture that has largely come to treat and regard music more as a commodity to be sold and profited from rather than simply a form of communication and expression available for the mutual enrichment and upliftment of all.

As a result, much of the messaging and Health of the music that we may be exposed to has become diluted, lost, or downright rotten. This brings me to my next question.

## What is Health?

Let's see what we might find when we look up the word health in a dictionary. Here are two of the ways Merriam-Webster's Dictionary defines *health*: (1) "the condition of being sound in body, mind, or spirit" and (2) "the general condition of the body."

For me, there is only Health with an uppercase H. When I ask myself, "What is Health?" some words and concepts come to mind, such as "well-being," "sound constitution," and "harmony." Health also seems to imply a sense of vigor and a strong life force. It has the ring of abundance and empowerment to it. It simply feels good. To be Healthy for me means to stand in a mutually beneficial relationship between (1) myself and myself, (2) myself and other, and (3) myself and the Universe.[2]

---

[2] *Feel free to substitute the word Universe for God, Higher Self, Creator, The All That Is, or whichever term makes you feel best. For me, Universe feels the most . . . well, universal.* ☺

From a Health standpoint, what is perhaps the clearest connection to the concept of music if not the critically important bodily phenomenon of homeostasis? When homeostasis is operating well, all the various organs, tissues, muscles, and systems in our body work together in wonderful concert – like a beautifully conducted symphony orchestra. In a truly Healthy human being, there is a sense of unity, harmony, and an amazingly coherent collaboration between all the various and diverse components working together.

The term *Healthy* also seems to indicate mutual benefit between multiple parties and a sense of thriving and cooperative co-existence between the various forces of life and its environment. Many of us live in an environment that is saturated by music in one way or another. I am compelled to wonder how such music saturation affects the overall Health of humanity (especially when my heart and gut tell me that a lot of the easy-access music in widespread circulation is of questionable value to human Health). As I see it, the question then becomes the following.

### Is There a Link Between Music and Health?

As a musician with over two decades of experience, I can say with utmost certainty, YES! Allow me to share from personal experience as to some of the ways that I began to feel confident in this link between music and Health.

## Beautiful Music And Vibrant Health Are Harmonious

When I was in high school, I remember wondering to myself, "How do the other kids in school who don't engage with music survive?" At that time, I could not even imagine how I could manage to get through the muck and the mire of daily existence without being able to release or alchemize my challenging emotions through either listening to my favorite music or playing and creating my own music.

In music, I had found that special something to look forward to and occupy my mind with when negative thoughts arose vying to try and fill my head. Music was an invaluable catharsis and release for me. So even from a young age, I understood that there was something very significant about the power of music, certainly in my life and from what I could tell, in the lives of many people that I knew.

As I wondered how some people got by without music playing a significant role in their lives, I noticed something else. I saw that there were a lot of frustrated and angry people around me who seemed stuck in their frustration and anger, while I eventually moved beyond being regularly absorbed by those unsatisfying energies to become a primarily mellow and contented person. Undoubtedly, multiple factors influenced my personal evolution. Still, I knew that in large part, it had something to do with how deeply meaningful, inspirational, and life-affirming music was as a force in my life (and, by contrast, perhaps not in the lives of the others who had, from my point of view, remained stuck).

As I got older, I reflected on my life experience and realized that when I listened to angry, more aggressive music, I tended to feel heavier, introverted, and darker. On the other hand, when I listened to more pure, beautiful, and harmonious music, I felt lighter, more inspired to connect with others, and generally happier. The link between music and my Health was clear to me.

I also saw this reflected in the lives of my guitar students. For a long time, I exposed my students to the same rock and metal music that had inspired me as a youth, as I was not yet fully aware of its potentially negative energy. Later, as I began to recommend music to my students with a bit more wisdom and careful judgment, I noticed a difference in the way these students developed both as guitarists and as human beings. I had begun to realize that it was important for myself and those in my sphere of influence to be both well-informed about the power of music and empowered to choose music that was Healthy and inspiring.

In the following pages, I'd like to share my conviction that making the connection between one's Health and how music either contributes to or detracts from it is a worthwhile endeavor. In making and understanding this connection, we can be empowered to create a more harmonious and fulfilling life on all levels.

## Intuitive Questions

*What springs to mind when you think of the word "music"?*

*What springs to mind when you think of the word "Health"?*

*Do you naturally feel that there is a connection between music and Health?*

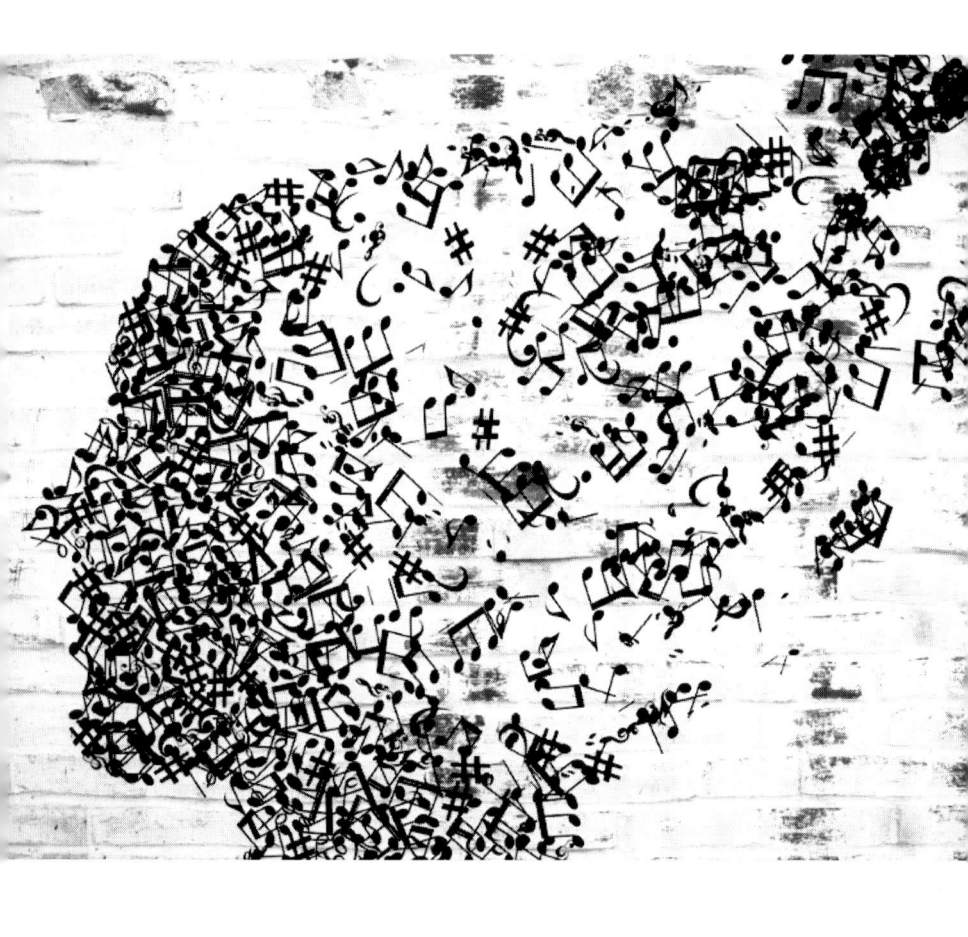

CHAPTER 2

# WHY IS THE *MIND YOUR MUSIC* CONVERSATION RELEVANT?

For the sake of simplicity, I will speak in generalizations to make my point in this chapter. So, let's zoom out and away from music for a few paragraphs and focus instead on the macro-level of where I perceive our collective human society stands in all its beauty, weaknesses, and fragility at this present time in history.

## Some Advantages of Modern Technology

The level of technology[3] in our current digital and information age allows for the creation of many wonderful new opportunities for individuals and humankind and offers a host of useful and wonderful tools to us. Here are but a few examples of its advantages:
- Computers, smartphones, and the internet connect us with family, friends, and new people the world over.

---

3  I use the term technology here in its broader sense of technical knowledge used to solve problems, accomplish specific objectives, and invent tools. While I am not speaking only of electronics, of course I am also implying them (e.g., computers, smart phones, and the like which are commonly associated with the word technology).

- Many jobs can now be done from the comfort of one's own home, thanks to the marvels of the internet and the ubiquity of capable devices.
- Supermarkets can conveniently provide enormous amounts of food thanks to various technologies.
- You can go food shopping or order a meal from and to your own home through your phone or computer.
- Cars, buses, trains, planes, and various other vehicles take us hither and thither at rates of travel generally much quicker than was possible just a century ago.
- So many creature comforts are made in mass quantities and obtainable even by those in lower-income thresholds.
- Internet platforms make it easy to access vast amounts of music, videos, and video games, among other entertainments and diversions.
- Internet shopping brings a whole new level of convenience to the consumer.
- Artists and content creators have more tools than ever at their disposal, allowing for a sort of Renaissance in creativity and expression.
- Social media can make beautiful connections between people possible, help develop friendships, and spread worthy and humane causes.

As we can see, modern technology does indeed color our lives in many extraordinary, convenient, and useful ways.

## Some Disadvantages of Modern Technology

Our current level of technology also creates an imbalance that, left unchecked, can veer us into some potentially catastrophic territory. While there may be numerous benefits to having access to the enormous amount of entertainment, pleasure, and opportunities to create and consume that we enjoy in much of the world today, this also leaves us open to a dark and unsavory side of life when potentially helpful restraints are absent in the face of these newly found powers.

Here are some examples of highly questionable uses of technological privilege that come to mind:

- Hate groups can unite through websites.
- Tutorials about bombs and weapons are posted online.
- Fear-mongering platforms can and do exist which feed on the unprotected energies of innocent people.
- Pornography sites are ubiquitous, contributing to normalizing warped and unnatural behaviors.
- Social media contributes to a great deal of depression and anxiety, especially in young people.
- Thanks to the unchecked wonders of modern technology, the vast, often cruel, and inhumane factory farming industry can flourish.
- Megastores that maximize technological advantages to take over markets around the world often put local mom-and-pop shops in a position where they are forced to close. At the same time, the new jobs

created by these same megastores tend to be relatively limited in terms of opportunities to develop skills and earning potential.
- Many large chain stores now employ self-checkout services, which often require human assistance anyway! Not only are the number of employees reduced by this use of technology, but employees who remain may not be incentivized nor sincerely encouraged to develop their talents and abilities through the human connection of sincere and caring mentors.
- Many if not most email inboxes receive an endless barrage of spam emails, which can be viewed as an invasion of our mental and emotional space and time.
- Junk paper mail (also made possible by unhindered use of technology, if a bit more dated) can pile up at one's residence, leaving us to wonder about the waste of paper, ink, and time.
- Web-crawling bots leave unrelated comments on website blogs promoting certain businesses while disregarding the true spirit of the websites they abuse. For example, In the comments section of the blog page on my website, I have had to waste time sorting through and deleting many spam comments, a waste of my time, energy, and attention.
- Unwelcome and unpleasant scam robocalls have been a continuing and constant nuisance in recent years.

These are just some examples that demonstrate the disadvantages of having knowledge, power, and resources without a strong sense of moral, social, and ecological responsibility. I could go on, and I imagine you might be able to think of other ways technology is not being used to benefit the greater good.

## Profit and "Progress" Over People

When our natural right to personal enrichment is confused with unbounded self-interest, the gateway is opened to the unfolding of any number of unfortunate circumstances to which mainstream news headlines on any given day are a constant attestation. If you look at our modern world, sadly, you can see parts of it that thrive in a state of greed and profit-over-people models.

Unfortunately, it can seem that much of our current human population still lives under a paradigm where financial profit and "progress" are prioritized above Health and human harmony. We are constantly bombarded with obnoxious advertising and marketing messages in almost every form of media we consume. Whether we are interacting on social media, watching a television show or movie, reading a magazine or newspaper, or surfing the internet, it is easy to get lost in the confusion of it all. And all this content reaches our eyes and ears, and those of highly impressionable youth, countless times per day. We are often subjected to promotions that encourage us to follow the mainstream and live in pursuit of the same short-sighted and unsustainable life paths that so many celebrities and people in the public eye pursue and even explicitly condone. This is the water in which we all swim. I believe it is crucial to understand and be aware of this aspect of our shared reality. Otherwise, we risk inadvertently normalizing this state of affairs by accepting it as "just the way it is." I am reminded of Albert Einstein when he said, "It has become appallingly clear that our technology has surpassed our humanity. I hope that someday, our humanity might yet surpass our technology."

I suggest that using our vast technological privileges works best when combined with a sense of social and ecological responsibility and a spirit of altruism. If, instead, it is used with an unrestrained attitude of "I'll do as I like, regardless of the consequences," the value of these privileges can become lost in destructive behaviors that are harmful to others and our world.

## We Are What We Consume

Are you familiar with the phrase "You are what you eat"? It makes sense, right? If you are putting certain foods into your body, then it stands to reason that those foods are the same raw materials that are building your body, and, therefore, your body will be made up of the raw materials you've provided to it. I'd like to expand on that logic to show how it also applies to many other areas of our lives, including music, by rephrasing it to "We are what we consume." The word "consume" has a broader meaning than the word "eat." In this context, *consumption* refers to anything we put into our mind-body-spirit system, whether by eating, drinking, listening, watching, absorbing, smelling, tasting, learning, believing, or by any other conceivable mode of doing so. Consumption also means *purchasing*, which seems very appropriate as we live in a consumer culture. Many of us define ourselves by the things that we *buy* (consume) rather than what we *create* ourselves. Consumers are dependent upon creators and manufacturers. Each human being is capable of both creating and consuming. How each one of us creates and consumes will be unique to each one of us. Rather than just accepting pre-selected content and materials to consume at appointed times, one simple creative power that we can each exercise is choosing how, what, and when we consume in light of how we want to experience our life.

I've learned this lesson of "we are what we consume" over and over in my life. For example, I loved watching (consuming) horror movies during my teen and young adult years. In those days, I also had many nightmares that sometimes made me feel like I was paralyzed and couldn't wake up. This went on for years, and I wondered, "Why is this happening?" Somehow, I finally got the hint to stop watching horror movies, and guess what? The nightmares went away. Surprising? Not really.

Similarly, for many years I listened to (consumed)

heavy and aggressive music and found myself unconsciously feeling angry and withholding my trust and love from people. As I slowly began shifting the music and content I consumed to a lighter, brighter variety, I also started to lighten up and allow people into my life on a deeper level. I began removing the blocks that I had built around my own heart. I realized that it wasn't that other people were inherently cold or untrustworthy. Instead, I was pushing them away by my attitudes, unconscious beliefs, and outward behaviors. When I changed my tastes and started consciously being aware of and filtering the content that I put into my ears, eyes, mind, and heart, my relationship with the people and the world around me expanded for the better.

    I began to truly understand that when I was living unconsciously and unquestioningly as a consumer, I was giving away some of my precious power as a sovereign being. By acknowledging how sensitive I am to what I consume in all realms of my life: music, movies, media, food, and more, I felt empowered to find healthier, lighter, and brighter materials to consume so I could become a healthier, lighter, and more radiant human being. For many years now, I have followed this logic, and it works for me.

    If you are in a place that feels a bit heavy and dark, this approach can have the same effect on you. You don't need to rush in and flip your life upside down overnight. Please don't! Instead, you can simply begin the process of minding your music. A simple step might be, next time you are about to put on some music, just pause and ask yourself this question, "How do I intend to feel as a result of listening to this music?" You don't even need to answer the question. The simple act of reflecting and acknowledging the power that music holds to influence your mood will plant an important seed.

## Proactive Rather Than Reactive

In short, I believe that the *mind your music* conversation is so relevant today because, as a society, we are at a crisis point regarding our Health on many levels. Just listening to the daily news broadcasts or reading the headlines of mainstream newspapers and media, it is plain to see that, as a species, we have room for improvement. It's easy to become overwhelmed and feel pessimistic after hearing so much bad news. How many times must we hear about environmental disasters, human and animal rights violations, pandemics, physical and mental health crises, mass shootings, suicides, wars, and many more unpleasant things existing in our world before we decide to commit to (at the very least) improving the state of our *own* life?

Ok, bad stuff happens every day. We get it. How can we focus on empowering ourselves to be proactive change-makers rather than reactive and scared slaves to a flawed system that is bound to evolve out of its current shape anyway? We can see so obviously that many human beings have forgotten or lost sight of their inherent nobility and natural-born right to lead a joyful and healthy life. So many people live in this type of reactivity mode, simply accepting their lot in life, so to speak.

    I strongly believe that being proactive in living our lives is a far richer, more pleasant, and more rewarding experience of being alive. How can we escape fear if we refuse to acknowledge our power as co-creators of our shared reality? When we step into our power as co-creators, we can make choices that reflect the healthier, lighter, and brighter world in which most of us prefer to live. There are countless ways that we can be co-creators of our reality. **I believe music can play a crucial role in balancing our relationship with ourselves, our world, and our environment.**

    In the next chapter, we'll take a closer look at some of the many ways that music can enrich our lives. As you read on, I encourage you to consider how valuable music is in your own life and how you can, or already do, have a healthy and balanced relationship with it.

## Intuitive Questions

*Can you think of some advantages of modern technology?*

*Can you think of some disadvantages of modern technology?*

*What comes to mind when you ponder the phrase "We are what we consume"?*

*Do you prefer to be proactive or reactive in your own life?*

# CHAPTER 3

# MUSIC CAN ENRICH OUR LIVES

Would you like to enrich your life? Who wouldn't? Perhaps you have several go-to methods and approaches that you use to contribute positive energy and a sense of balance to your life? You may even use music in many enriching ways already. If you do, perhaps this chapter title sounds a bit obvious to you. And if you do not, then I hope it sparks something useful for you. In either case, I'd like to go into a bit of detail as to some of the various ways music can enrich our lives.

## Rethinking the Role and Value of Music

There is a common adage that goes something like this: "You don't know what you have until it is gone." Along my path of life, I have experienced this. However, I have also benefitted from doing small meditations or thought experiments to help me gain an appreciation for things that I feel I may be taking for granted at any given time. Before we explore together some of the various ways music can enrich our lives, I suggest we take a brief pause.

[ [ [ . . . p a u s e . . . ] ] ]

Ok, thank you! I now invite you to participate in two brief thought experiments with me simply to deepen our appreciation and estimation of music itself. Let's ponder the following two questions together:

*What would human life be without music?*

What if we did not have the capacity to conceive of constructing musical equipment or if we weren't capable of learning how to sing or play? Imagine how different the world would be! Try spending a day, a week, or a month without experiencing any music at all. I am sure you will notice there's a difference in your enjoyment and experience of life. Perhaps bearing this thought experiment in mind may help us bring a more conscious appreciation of the power of music in our lives.

*What if we thought of music as a magical gift from the Universe to humanity?*

It is my belief and experience that music truly is a precious treasure freely provided to us by the Universe as conscious beings to be enjoyed, shared, and used as a tool to enrich the lives of everybody on our planet (and beyond) regardless of our many differences. If it feels like a stretch to talk about music with such high regard, perhaps just humor me and try it on for a moment?

When music is genuinely honored, there is no limit to the beauty, connection, inspiration, and sense of togetherness that it can create. However, when music is perverted and treated without a sense of dignity, respect, and gratitude, it can quickly become a dark force that divides us and blocks us off from one another. It can send us down roads of trivial and superficial pursuits that often generate unHealthy beliefs about ourselves, others, and the world around us.

I sometimes feel that music is essential to life, like water or air. In my view, for most humans, it is a vital element for living a rich and full life. If, and when, we freely choose to adopt the view that music is a magical gift given to us by the Universe, wouldn't it be fitting to honor it with the full respect that such a powerful and beautiful gift deserves?

I present the remainder of this chapter in six general categories as a broad overview of some diverse ways in which music has the potential to enrich human life. I do not cite specific sources within the text, but if you would like to dive deeper into some of the information mentioned below, have a look in "Additional Resources" towards the back of the book, which includes links to relevant articles, videos, books and more.

## Children, Parenthood, and Education

For anyone who has any experience with children, it would be no surprise for me to say that children like music. Children's music can be an effective communicator of basic language learning, core values, and everyday activities. We all know some of the very basics that help us to learn our native tongue. In English, we have "The Alphabet Song," which teaches children the alphabet in a way most of us will never forget. There are many songs, for example, that teach core human values about loving one another, loving ourselves, working together, and respecting our differences. One such popular song is "It's a Small World." There are also many songs about everyday activities such as brushing teeth, cleaning up, exercising, or going to sleep. Of course, many children's songs are simply silly and fun, which promotes laughter and a good mood.

For babies, music can be beneficial at as early a stage as in the womb. Some mothers play classical music for their unborn babies to soothe and calm them. Once born, music can help babies fall asleep – just think of any number of lullabies. As a father, I can attest to music's usefulness in child development. Music can help children to calm down when they've become overly excited and to play happily by creating a good mood. As children learn and imitate basic rhythms, they strengthen their ability to learn, comprehend, and communicate.

In the field of education, music advocates often tout the benefits of music programs to enhance learning and developmental skills for school children. Studies have revealed that students who participate in music programs have shown increased focus and perception, improved cognitive function, enhanced visual and verbal skills, as well as ability to participate in teamwork. All of which can lead to higher academic achievement and social skills.

## Physical Fitness and Wellness

It is perhaps well known that music can motivate us when we work out. Many workout videos incorporate music to bring energy to the exercise. In gyms, you may hear upbeat music playing over the loudspeakers or see gym members wearing earbuds while working out. People going for a walk or a run often use music to have something to listen to and engage them as they move.

Sometimes music may be the key ingredient to inspire us to do the workout in the first place. In other words, it can make the difference in deciding whether to work out or not. As a jogger, I can attest to how effective music has been in motivating me to go out and have a good run. Energizing and inspirational music has the capacity also to encourage us to exercise longer and more vigorously.

One of the reasons music is such a great companion for exercise is because it encourages rhythmical movement and synchronized breathing patterns, which enhance aerobic capabilities. That's why music with a strong beat is the driving force for dance-inspired exercises, like Zumba. For slower-paced exercises like yoga, a calming and atmospheric sound can significantly enhance both the physical activities and restorative qualities of the workout.

## Therapeutic and Healing Attributes

Have you ever had the experience of being roused out of a lousy mood into a good mood after hearing a piece of music that you love? Or have you ever felt a strong emotion such as sadness that was cathartically eased by listening to an excellent sad song? Music has the tremendously important power to help us release tension and transmute strong emotions while relieving stress and anxiety.

Listening to relaxing music is a simple and proven way to reduce stress by lowering blood pressure and calming our heart and breathing rate. These benefits are also helpful in reducing the risk of heart problems and preventing illness by increasing our body's immune response, improving our blood flow, and inspiring us to be calm and centered. Various forms of meditation can be assisted by appropriately calming and soothing soundscapes.

Music therapy is used to treat and care for all types of people, including those with autism, dementia, depression, and sleeping disorders. Therapeutic benefits of listening to music have been linked to promoting better sleep, relieving depression, improving interpersonal communication, stabilizing moods, and even easing pain.

In hospitals, patients often use music to help themselves relax before surgery and accelerate their healing process afterward. Using music to induce a meditative state has even been known to ease recovery in stroke patients.

Sound healing is an alternative healing modality that employs tones, soundscapes, and music to affect the body vibrationally positively.[4]

## Socializing and Greater Spiritual Connection

On a social level, music is truly a wonder of the world. It connects us instantaneously, crosses all boundaries, and bonds people from all over the world as mutual fans of one musical work or another. As they say, "Music is the universal language." Music is essential to any good party! It helps us relax and can encourage us to reach out and meet with people. Of course, it is the key ingredient to dancing, which is good for the body, the soul, *and* for socializing!

For musicians, music impels us to learn how to cooperate with one another (which is important for those of us who are not so social by nature!). It also teaches us how to express ourselves and have meaningful communications with others both with and without words.

Music helps people form bonds and connect by seeing that there is a larger world beyond ourselves and that we are a part of a larger community. For example, fans of the same song, musical artist, movie soundtrack,

---

4  See the final section of "Chapter 6 - Music as Magic" for more into on sound healing.

or video game soundtrack can experience an almost instant bond. Just look in the YouTube comments under one of your favorite inspirational songs or music videos, and you'll probably find many like-minded people whom you might even consider to be among your soul tribe.

Beyond the more practical aspects of the benefits of music, it also has a profound spiritual component. It can help create an atmosphere where people feel motivated to unite for a worthy cause or bring people together in lovely harmony for celebrations. Through the amazing act of singing (both alone and together), music enables us to express deep feelings and emotions that may have difficulty finding expression any other way.

In sports, at any age or level, music has the power to help people perform better in high-pressure situations. Just think about how a pep band, crowds chanting a musical phrase, or sports fans singing at a stadium, have a powerful ability to rally team spirits and inspire the players to perform at their best. When I played little league baseball, I would feel a surge of renewed determination joining my teammates to sing a song to cheer us up when we were lagging in the game.

Music can assist us with tapping into our family roots which can help us get in touch with ourselves and our ancestry on a profound level. For example, I've been listening to traditional Irish music since I was a little boy. The music imparted to me Irish culture, character, and to some extent, an addition to my personal identity, which suited me. Without this family tradition and association,

I would have only a vague sense of what being part-Irish means to me as I have not yet been to Ireland and have never had any contact with relatives from there. Largely because of my early love for Irish music, my curiosity about and interest in my Irish ancestry has remained with me throughout my life.

## Deep Listening

True communication begins with deep and conscious listening. Because music greatly improves our ability to focus and listen closely, it naturally makes us better and deeper listeners. Have you ever noticed how rare it is to find someone who deeply listens to what you say? Can you imagine a world where deep listening is common practice? In contrast to conversations between people who are simply waiting for the other person to stop talking so they can speak, conversations between people engaged in deep listening naturally result in a much more meaningful and fulfilling exchange.

Developing the power of truly and consciously listening to music helps us realize what it means to be present to the diversity of human expression. We can extend this practice into our daily interactions with the world around us and the people we meet. Listening to others is not only a wonderful gift to be freely given, but it may well be one of the most crucial skills to learn at this unique time in our history. As pressing global concerns continue to surface in our planetary collective consciousness, it is necessary now more than ever to take meaningful action utilizing deep listening to build mutual trust and broaden understanding between our diverse global communities. Conscious listening to high-quality music can be a powerful ally in building the bridges needed to create mutual understanding and compassion across the globe.

From the various examples above, I hope you can see some of the numerous ways that music can and indeed does enrich our lives all the time. When music is playing a Healthy role in society, everybody stands to benefit. So, is music playing a predominantly Healthy role in our society? That brings me to my next question for your consideration:

*Is ALL music beneficial and Healthy?*

## Intuitive Questions

*Can you imagine what your life
would be like without music?*

*As an exercise, can you accept that music
is a magical gift from the Universe to humanity?
If so, might this change your personal relationship
with music in any way?*

*Have you ever experienced a fitness activity
that was enhanced by music?*

*Have you ever experienced stress relief, relaxation,
or other physical improvements to your state of being
in connection to the music you were listening to?*

*Have you ever sensed a connection between
consistent musical activity and strong mental capacity
either in yourself or someone you know?*

*Do you have memories in your life when a social
situation was made more fun, enjoyable, and
meaningful due to music being involved?*

*Do you believe that being listened to deeply
(in dialogue) is a gift (to be both given and received)?*

# CHAPTER 4

## THE SLIDING SCALE OF UNHEALTHY TO HEALTHY MUSIC

Now that we are aware of the power of music and how much it influences our lives, I'd like to get into the nitty-gritty of how we, as consumers (and creators) of music, can think about and roughly categorize the music in our lives. To that end, I offer the following concept for your consideration. Namely, that all music fits into one of three general categories on a sliding spectrum: *unHealthy music*, *gray music*, and *Healthy music*.

**UnHealthy Music**

Truly unHealthy music is easy to notice. It tends to be very disrespectful, often violent in nature, very aggressive, very dark. The lyrics tend to be poisonous and clearly are not intended to uplift the human spirit but rather denigrate it. You will very likely not feel good when you listen to this kind of music, and it might leave you with a general sense of depression, fear, anxiety, even nausea.

My view may be a bit subjective, but I am speaking plainly from experience. There is music out there that is just flat-out demeaning, disrespectful, violence-promoting, derogatory, offensive, sometimes prejudiced, and downright hateful. I can say with complete confidence that any music that falls into this category is unHealthy and actually has the power to corrupt minds and make you physically and mentally sick!

However, even in the general unHealthy category, there is a significant amount of gray music that may have some social or musical value that sets it apart. For example, some music may be super aggressive and borderline violent yet makes a significant social statement and may be worth the occasional, very conscious listen. Similarly, music that may be very dark lyrically might have incredible musicianship making it worth listening to occasionally for that purpose (if you can consciously tune out the lyrical messaging). In either case, please exercise caution when dabbling in listening to this type of music, so you don't unconsciously absorb toxic and negative energies.

Here is an example of what I would personally consider unHealthy music. In my late teens, I went to an aggressive heavy metal show at the Roseland Ballroom (New York City). I was not a huge fan of the band, but at the time, I felt that it was part of my social duty as a "metalhead" to check out the occasional crazy concert experience. While part of me loved attending live shows, my general sense even then was that rock concerts were often way too loud and perhaps a bit too reckless to be considered a very Healthy environment. But this particular show was bone-crushingly loud, and the energy was very dark and aggressive no matter where I was in the crowd.[5] As I wandered around the venue trying to find a semi-comfortable and safe place to watch the show, I saw two full-fledged fistfights break out near me. I'm talking about the kinds of fights where the ambulance gets involved. I became sick to my stomach from the negative energy and ended up leaving the concert early in disgust.

In my view, unHealthy music[6] can be compared to taking drugs or abusing alcohol. If you're not exercising extreme caution and discipline with this stuff, it can very subtly and quickly pull you into a downward spiral. So, for many people, not dabbling in listening to unHealthy music at all may be the wisest choice.

**Gray Music**

Gray music is what it sounds like, a mix between Healthy and unHealthy music. Most of the music

---

5  This is not an argument against all aggressive music shows. I understand aggressive music shows can have a positive mental health and social aspect that gives people an outlet to express themselves in a very deep way that cannot easily be found elsewhere. However, this particular show I am referring to (and shows like it) demonstrates one type of dark energy atmosphere that I definitely did not enjoy being in nor would I recommend to anyone.

6  As a seeker of truth and true lover of music I cannot help but remain open-minded to all forms of music at least to some extent. I do generally give things a try before making a personal judgement. For me to continue listening to something, it's important that it gives me a good vibe personally.

available to the public falls into this category, and, at times, it may be enjoyable. You may think, "Ok, the lyrics are a bit negative, and there is some strong language, but the music is *really* good, and I enjoy listening to it." Or vice versa, "The lyrics are great, but the music is a bit too aggressive for my tastes."

When this happens, I encourage you to use wisdom in making your choice about listening to this type of music. Take the music for what it is and either listen to it or don't listen to it. The important thing is to be aware and listen consciously so that you can choose what to accept and what to release.

If you listen unconsciously, the toxic elements in gray music will have a much better chance of seeping into your brain and possibly leaving an unsavory presence that can sap your life force.

You may think that is not so bad, but if you continuously listen to a lot of this type of music, it has the power to slowly but surely, pollute your life and cloud your thoughts in an unHealthy way. A good comparison might be what happens when you consume nutrient-deficient junk food every day without seriously considering whether there might be a downside to it or exploring healthier alternatives and begin to have health problems of one sort or another.

A classic example of gray music from my life occurred one evening during my college days at the music conservatory. I was wandering the hallways at night as I tended to do from time to time and came

## The Sliding Scale Of UnHealthy to Healthy Music

across a somewhat odd and depressed fellow student and musician. We initially struck up a conversation around some of the classical music we were studying and eventually moved on to talking about our favorite music.

We agreed on our mutual fandom of two bands in the new wave genre. However, before I could get carried away with praising the cathartic merits of these bands, my new acquaintance explained that listening to these and similar bands too much had become counterproductive for him. He said that although he experienced an initial euphoric joy when listening to this type of music, it eventually led him into an isolated and cynical inner state of being that increased (rather than curtailed) his tendency towards feeling depressed. So, for him, listening to this particular type of music had become an unHealthy experience.

For myself, however, I had not over-indulged in listening to this type of music, and my overall disposition was relatively balanced at the time. So, I found the music beneficial (Healthy) to listen to in small doses.

This conversation was an eye-opener to me and revealed what I had long suspected but had not been ready to face – our music-consuming choices do indeed have a significant impact on our Health, and that each of us as individuals will have our own unique degree of sensitivity to the energy of any particular music.

Another example of how tricky gray music can be occurred one evening in my late 20's while on a car ride to Long Island with some friends. We got together just to get out and have fun exploring someplace new. As the organizer of this somewhat motley crew of different personalities, I felt responsible for how well everyone got along. Even though I had no ability, nor desire, to control my group of friends in any way, I knew that the type of energy I brought to the situation through music could influence the atmosphere and affect the overall group dynamic.

It was around Halloween, and I could not resist the temptation to blast some dark heavy metal music known for being spooky and even demonic. In the past, my friends and I had enjoyed listening to this music many times without any noticeably negative consequences (though generally, in those experiences, we were younger, more aggressive, and less sensitive in some respects). But this time, as I turned on the cassette tape, I sensed it was a calculated risk that could potentially derail the good vibes in the car. Something inside warned me that this might not be a wise choice since not everyone in this group knew each other, and some were not particularly fans of this type of music. But I was a fan of the band and wanted to create a Halloween-like atmosphere, so I went for it.

Almost immediately, the music seemed to alter the atmosphere. Although it was kind of cool at first, before long, some of my friends began to bicker with each other. This kind of behavior was not terribly unusual when hanging out with diverse friends at that time in my

## The Sliding Scale Of UnHealthy to Healthy Music

life, but typically the disputes resolved quickly. However, this time, the bickering did not stop and lingered on as an unpleasant vibe that lasted throughout the rest of the car ride. I tried to improve the vibe by changing the music to something more mellow and peaceful, but it was too late. The damage had been done. The experience was so disturbing that I decided to end our trip early to get away from the nasty vibe.

I was tempted to blame the immaturity of my friends for the bad experience, but, intuitively, I knew I had unintentionally contributed to creating a toxic environment by blasting that energetically dark heavy metal music. I wondered if things would have been different had I chosen beautiful classical music or any other type of uplifting and positive-vibe music. Would that have steered the energy of the group in a more congenial and friendly direction? Perhaps there is no definitive answer, but I suspect we would have had a very different evening altogether had I chosen other music to set the tone. In retrospect, it was a helpful experience that truly deepened my convictions about the influence, both positive and negative, of music in our day-to-day lives.

Now, let's broadly consider the gray music genres of heavy metal and hard rock music. In heavy metal music, much of the lyrical content (not all) tends toward pessimistic, destructive, angry, and perhaps even demonic themes, yet the songs themselves do not necessarily advocate negative behaviors but rather focus on painting a stark picture of some aspect of perceived reality. Many hard rock songs, by comparison, tend to be very sex-oriented, rebellious (for their own sake), or promote a self-indulgent, party-hard lifestyle.[7] Yet, despite the somewhat darker lyrical tone of these genres, much of this music may sound very appealing and cool.

The case is much the same in the gray music genres of hip-hop and rap. While songs in these genres often have catchy and energetic music, they also have similarly unHealthy lyrical themes glorifying sex, drugs, money, power, and, at times, even violence.

Perhaps surprisingly, in contrast to the generally pleasant sound of the music, some folk and country genres have fairly stark and hedonistic themes that also fall under the gray music category. While sad or rousing songs (commonplace in these genres) can have a healing and unifying quality in their proper place, these types of songs can also increase attachment to a limited identity that would be better outgrown. For example, if you have ever seen a person crying into his seventh beer while listening to the same sad song on loop, you get what I mean. Similarly, when a song about social injustice (in any genre) rouses a group of people to the point where they lose their compassion and love for

---

7 *I do not mean to oversimplify and create stereotypes regarding lyrics in the genres I mentioned, but I do think it's important to face the realities of the music that we consume without sugar-coating them. Of course, there will be numerous exceptions of non-stereotypical themes that can be found in virtually all genres.*

their fellow man and instead direct their energies toward seeking vengeance and destruction, this is also out of balance and unhelpful (unHealthy).

Another significant and somewhat more subtle example of gray music is the vast commercial world of pop and dance music. Many songs in these categories are about romantic love, sex, revenge, rebellion, being larger-than-life, or other themes that dramatize and hyper-focus on relatively shallow elements of day-to-day reality. When taken out of context or overexposed to this type of music, the human brain can be driven crazy with imbalanced concerns about one's external image, material gain, popularity, or shallow relationships that have little or nothing to do with the deepest most enduring aspects of living a truly abundant life (e.g., self-worth, unconditional love, compassion, contributing value, and building peaceful communities).

Pop music may play an important role in our society, but it can also distort daily life priorities through lyrics that inflate and exaggerate concerns about self-image and the ego-self, which may be way out of proportion to reality. To let loose and have fun, a little bit at a time, may contribute to a Healthy lifestyle, but I strongly urge you to be aware of how much of this type of music you let into your life and be cognizant of how it is *truly* making you feel.

I often compare pop music to eating junk food, smoking cigarettes, social drinking, or consuming soda pop. It may all seem harmless enough. After all, "It's good for parties and, at least, it's better than hard drugs, right?" While this may be true to a degree, in excess, pop music can be harmful. Consider that pop music, like most all music, has a certain hypnotic quality that can affect your state of mind. Careless listening to this type of music (or any gray music for that matter) can cause you to buy into the shallow and unrealistic messages in these songs, leaving you feeling drained and craving another pick-me-up.

Pop music also drives materialistic culture and consumerism in a similar way that junk food does. One potato chip is never enough, is it? While eating chips may seem to help you get by in the moment, eating too many over prolonged periods is unHealthy. Similarly, overconsumption of this type of music can be detrimental, especially when you are unconsciously listening to it. When allowing this music to infiltrate our lives without putting our healthy personal filters in place, we run the risk of unwittingly taking on beliefs and behaviors that are not only unHealthy but also not even our own.

**Healthy Music**

Like unHealthy music, truly Healthy music is also easy to notice. You can definitely tell if you feel uplifted, joyful, merry, peaceful, or any number of positive moods or states of being.

You know when a song makes you feel really good. You can sense the change in your own body chemistry.

## The Sliding Scale Of UnHealthy to Healthy Music

You can feel yourself coming alive in a good way. You may want to run, jump, cry, sing, dance, work, smile, call someone, or simply relish in the joy of being alive. You know music is Healthy if it boosts your spirits or inspires a feeling of peace and well-being. It may also make you want to expand your life in a Healthy way. For example, you may listen to a certain piece of music that inspires you to want to take a leisurely stroll in nature.

Healthy music may inspire your imagination, help you to relax or concentrate more deeply. It may pique your curiosity about other cultures and the world at large. It may make you want to connect with other people and experience life. Healthy music fascinates you and ignites your passion for seeing the depths of mystery and beauty in the world.

At some point in my late teens or early twenties, I was looking through my mother's CD (compact disc) collection to find some new listening material. I was open to expanding my tastes and looking for something lighter than the emotionally and sonically heavy music that I normally listened to. One of the CDs I selected from my mom's collection called *Down to the Moon*[8] caught my attention due to its unusual and otherworldly album art.

I played the CD and was immediately struck by the sound of the music. "What on Earth is this?" I wondered. Was I hearing an orchestra of sorts? Was this all

---

8  Andreas Vollenweider – *Down to the Moon* (1986)

done with electronic synthesizers? Was it all MIDI?[9] I honestly had no idea, and the sparse liner notes for the album, as well as the absence of photos, left a lot to my imagination. I allowed myself to be immersed in a sound journey hoping against hope that the magic I heard in the first few seconds would continue throughout the album. All too often, I would experience albums that had snippets of magic followed by mediocrity. *Down to the Moon,* however, delivered on its promise to transport me to another world. Once this sonic journey began, it captivated me right through until the last notes were played and the CD came to a stop.

I fell in love with this album and listened to it from beginning to end countless times in the years that followed. The whole journey is so magical that I never felt compelled to learn the names of any of the individual tracks. For me, there is only *Down to the Moon.* Many times, when life was weighing heavy on me in my young adulthood, I would give myself permission to just lie down in bed with the lights off and allow the sound of this beautiful and mystical music to wash over me and energetically cleanse my life. While I didn't fully realize it at the time, I was allowing myself to undergo self-administered sound healing[10] sessions. And it worked.[11]

---

9 *MIDI (Musical Instrument Digital Interface) is a technical standard in digital music. Rather than actual instruments being played and recorded, MIDI can be used as a substitute to simulate these electronically.*
10 *For a further discussion on sound healing, see "Chapter 6 - Music as Magic" towards the end of the chapter.*
11 *Fortunately, there is quite a lot of good quality Healthy music*

## The Sliding Scale Of UnHealthy to Healthy Music

Christmas carols are also an excellent example of Healthy music. I don't mean to say that *all* Christmas music is Healthy – a lot of it is just commercial nonsense, in my opinion, but music that is truly about honoring the good in the world while spreading cheer and glad tidings is clearly of the Healthier variety.

During one Christmas season in my mid-20's, I took part in a church choir for about a month. One day after work, I dropped into a nearby Catholic church on a whim. The church choir was practicing, and it sounded beautiful. I learned that the choir was looking for more singers for a Christmas midnight mass performance that included a rendition of Handel's "Hallelujah" Chorus. I felt moved by the magic of the moment and offered to sing in the choir for this special event.

The next few weeks of singing practice were interesting and inspirational. The event itself was truly beautiful. There were so many people eagerly listening and singing along in the congregation. The feeling of participating in and co-creating sacred music meant to uplift, inspire, and soothe the soul was a highlight amongst my many diverse musical experiences. Even though I no longer identified as Catholic (at the time, I was actively seeking the religion that most deeply resonated with me), I could not deny the Healthy, life-affirming, and wholesome vibe of the music in the

---

*available out there for you to explore in your own life. (See "John Henry's Recommended Listening List" and "Additional Resources" towards the back of this book for some listening ideas).*

church that Christmas night.

Along the spectrum of unHealthy to Healthy music, there is also a light-gray music sub-category within Healthy music that is based on personal tastes and preferences. There will be songs that may make *you* feel great, but perhaps others will disagree or vice versa. Then there are those songs that *really make you feel great* despite the perhaps dark or hedonistic mental level of the lyrical message. These are usually found in the gray music genres mentioned above, such as pop, dance, metal, rock, folk, country, hip-hop, rap, etc.[12] Again, you will have to trust your own judgment with songs like these.

It is not likely that everyone will agree on a definitive list of Healthy and unHealthy music. *So, what do we do?* How can we sort through the wide variety of musical choices that flow incessantly throughout our lives? In the next chapter, I will discuss some practical and intuitive steps you can take to help you find the music that is most resonant and complimentary to your life.

---

[12] *I am aware that the number of musical genres out there far exceeds the few that I discuss in this book. Please extend the guidelines that pertain to gray music to any music that may give you mixed messages. In other words, I encourage you to be aware of everything that you listen to and exercise good judgment as often as you remember to. Making conscious and informed choices about our music listening is the core message of this book.*

## Intuitive Questions

*Have you ever had a gut feeling about music being unHealthy for you or those in your environment?*

*Can you name a few artists or songs that come to mind for you when you think of unHealthy music?*

*Have you ever had a gut feeling about music being Healthy for you or those in your environment?*

*Can you name a few artists or songs that come to mind when you think of Healthy music?*

*Have you ever had a gut feeling that some of the music in your life is offering mixed messages and, on some level, clouding your thoughts and energies?*

*Can you name a few artists or songs that come to mind when you think of gray music?*

# CHAPTER 5

## HOW CAN YOU FIND THE BEST MUSIC FOR YOU?

As I've already suggested, it can sometimes seem that we live in a world of reckless abandon these days. Amidst all the confusion and chaos of our current media-saturated world, we are also constantly bombarded by music playing on the internet, TV, radio, movies, video games, and in shopping areas, restaurants, bars, airports. We even hear music on phone calls when we are put on hold.

In all the noise of the world, it can be challenging to decipher what music is worth listening to and what may be a waste of your time and energy. Further, the process itself of searching for and discovering good quality Healthy music also requires time and energy, which so many of us may feel like we lack in the quick pace of our modern lives. And what do we do about the various opinions of others? I may tell you one artist is great, while someone else may tell you the opposite or vice versa. All these various factors may leave us feeling overwhelmed and confused, wondering, "Isn't there a simpler way?"

While there is not a perfectly clear delineation of "good" and "bad" music that can be easily prescribed for *all* people, I can offer some helpful guidelines. Here are my recommendations for points to consider in choosing the right music for you.

## John Henry's Guidelines for Choosing the Best Music for Your Life

- Follow your instincts as to what music you *really* like.
- Observe your mood when you listen to the artists that you tend to listen to.
- How do you feel *while* you are listening to your favorite music?
- How do you feel shortly *after* you have listened to your favorite music?
- While listening to a piece of music, do you feel uplifted, peaceful, light-hearted, and generally good?
- While listening to a piece of music, do you feel sad, miserable, cold-hearted, angry, mistrustful, and generally bad?
- Does the music you listen to inspire you to want to reach out and connect with others?
- Does the music you listen to influence you to want to withhold, cut off, outshine, or even harm others?
- Notice patterns. Choose the music that supports you in feeling your best and start letting go of the music that makes you feel bad.
- Perhaps write out a list of your top 10 or 20 favorite songs that truly inspire you to feel great. Use this list as a guidepost and reference as you continue forward on your musical journey.

Finding the best music for your life also means expanding self-love and getting to know yourself in an ever-deepening way. Careful and honest observation of your moods whenever you listen to music will be one of the most accurate indicators for understanding how it is impacting your life. Naturally, there may also be value in listening to the opinions and recommendations of others. Still, I would like to emphasize that the *most* important element in what you choose to listen to is how *you* feel in the totality of your being when and after you experience it.

## How I Found the Best Music for Me

Coming to the place where I stand today in a Healthy relationship with the music in my life has been a rich and complex journey, no doubt. Allow me to share some examples of how applying the guidelines above worked for me along my journey.

During my youthful music-listening life, I really *loved* some artists whom my friends may have thought were "cheesy." Did I just forget about these artists to fit in with the crowd? No way! To this day, I still joyfully listen to some of these "cheesy" artists because they continue to affect my mood positively.[13]

---

[13] Over the years some of my naysaying friends have also changed their opinions about those same "cheesy" artists and now enjoy their music as well. I don't remind them of their former position though (*wink*) and manage to refrain from saying "I told you so."

When I was young, my mother frowned upon some of my favorite artists and songs, which gave me pause and made me second guess my choices a bit. I had to acknowledge that sometimes a particular music group or song I listened to may have had a vibe that was not aligned with *her* preferences. But when I looked deep inside myself and trusted *my own* heart and sense of joy, I mostly chose to remain a fan of the artist or song I liked. Despite what my dear mother's opinions may have been at the time, I mostly felt that the music I chose to listen to had more of a positive influence on me than a negative one. On occasion, her perspective did alter my view of certain music and was very helpful in encouraging me to honestly question the value and overall effect of the music in my life to find the best music for me.[14]

I am glad that I listened to my own heart and inner voice at such a young age in honoring my preferences because I know now that my heart is the truest and best guide for me to find music that compliments and enhances my life.[15] Whenever I have felt a deep

---

14 *It has always been important for me to at least acknowledge the opinions of others even if they are drastically different then mine. Putting human relationships as a high priority throughout my life has enabled me to stay grounded in who I am. By both standing firmly in my own truth while also allowing others to stand in their truth in a spirit of mutual respect I have been able to co-exist harmoniously and joyfully on this planet.*

15 *I feel compelled to also acknowledge the profound guiding effect of one's gut as well. In addition to my heart, listening to my gut has also steered me towards good situations and away from potentially very unpleasant ones time and again.*

connection and synergy with an artist, I took that to be a sign of a positive influence. After all, I believed that an artist-fan relationship was right for me if the music inspired me to feel good and have a better relationship with the world around me. This, in turn, inspired me to feel better and more passionate about my own life. In the instances where my mother's opinions were quite contrary to my own, I had quietly recognized that at the end of the day, the most important consideration for her was my Health and happiness. So, even if she didn't approve of all the music I was listening to as a youth (or later), she naturally came to accept our differences in musical opinion and allowed me to choose my own path without much resistance, especially when she saw that I was developing into a generally happy and Healthy young man.

Along my journey, I was able to sense the deeper truth and value in following my own heart. I noticed that much of the music I was choosing to listen to affected me in mainly positive ways. So, while I always tried to consider and respect the opinions of others, I continued to listen to the music that I loved. As I matured, so did my music choices.[16] I have listened to a lot of stuff that

---

[16] I have listened to a lot of gray area heavy metal music as a youth and thoroughly enjoyed it and grew from it at the time. I also know now where I personally stand with it considering my awareness of the potential toxicities of this gray music (which I may have been oblivious to at the time). Therefore, I might be hesitant to broadly recommend much of the music of my own youth to the youth of today as I can readily recognize the mixed messages and potentially negative influence in that music. Though, all things

I later realized was quite toxic, but at the time, was right for me. I firmly believe that you must trust *yourself* when choosing the music that is right for you. It's important to remember, too, that our musical tastes and listening needs are constantly evolving and to be open to making changes along the way.

## Sorting it All Out

So, what happens when you still have difficulty differentiating between which music has a good vibe for you and which has a bad vibe? How can you recognize the difference between Healthy and unHealthy music?

The *most* essential step is to learn to *trust yourself.* Go deep inside. Allow the music to be like a personal message composed just for you. If and when you feel moved, allow it. It may be a knee-jerk reaction for some people automatically to dislike music outside of their regular familiarity zone. Please don't be afraid to experiment and check out lots of different artists. By all means, do so! An open mind is essential for discovering the truth about anything. So, when exploring new music, try listening without judgment to hear the music truly and deeply, and then allow your heart, your gut, and your natural musical preferences to guide you forward.

---

*considered, for me the music of my youth played a crucial role in helping me to find my identity and in the development of my humanity. And significantly, part of the value in the music selections of my youth was that I sought them out on my own and developed my ability to listen to my inner guidance system in the process.*

Please be sure to also carry with you the awareness that your Health is at stake when you decide to stick with a certain type of music for the long haul. Regular exposure to the same music can significantly impact your frame of mind and your state of being – like creating a blueprint in your mind-body-spirit system.

Monitor yourself when you listen to music. How does your body feel? How is your mood affected by the music? Sometimes a song or genre that you used to like may become unenjoyable. And sometimes, a song that you formerly detested becomes appealing. It's ok—the process of evolution proceeds by allowing for the new and the unexpected. By continually tuning in to your heart, your gut, and your deep inner voice, you will discover and rediscover what music is right for you in each moment.

The road to discovering the best music for your life can be colorful and interesting. Throughout my extensive music-listening life, I've had quite a diverse range of experiences. There were times when I witnessed truly inspirational and beautiful music imbue an audience with a divine and sacred quality. I also recall countless times when the music brought the vibe up or engendered a sense of bonding among my family or friends (for example, thoughtfully selected gray area pop or rock music at a party). However, at other times, I found that playing uplifting light-gray music for the wrong crowd created an unharmonious atmosphere if the people present were fans of darker gray music.

And then there were even instances where I ended up having fights with my friends or family members shortly after listening to particularly aggressive or dark music![17]

It may be helpful to conduct your own research into artists that pique your interest and ask others for their opinions and suggestions. If an artist has a nasty reputation and a lot of controversy surrounding him or her, then perhaps that's an indicator of the type of energy that artist will bring into your life. And vice-versa, if the artist is widely known as being a kind-hearted and honest person with a loyal fan base, this might indicate that their music could potentially have a good influence on your life. In either case, knowing a little bit about the character and nature of a musical artist might be helpful. *What type of person(s) do you want filling your inner world with energy, ideas, and messages?* I believe it is a thought worth considering.

There are many forms of music out there, so there can be lots of exploring to do. I assure you that you will be able to find the music that contributes most beneficially to your life by tuning into your own senses and trusting your intuition about the artists that you are most genuinely drawn towards. You might explore the internet using search words that speak to the feelings you'd like to deepen and engender within yourself, such as "music to feel positive," "peaceful music," "dream music," "profound music," "feel-good music," and "light-

---

17 *In such a case, that was a pretty strong indicator for me that I was listening to unHealthy music.*

hearted music."[18] Adjectives and descriptive words that accurately describe what you are looking for can really help you hone in on the type of music you want. It has been my experience that if I am seeking something in my part of the world, there was a creator in another part of the world who created something which connects to my soul's craving. The same applies to you. If you are craving music with a particular sound or vibe, there is a strong likelihood it is out there waiting to be discovered. The world can be magical like that. Speaking of magic, that brings me to my next and final chapter - exploring the magic of music.

---

18 As a DIY (do-it-yourself) musical artist myself, I can tell you that a significant part of the music creator's world today involves using descriptive terms to describe one's music so that it can be found using text searches. In other words, artists are incentivized to connect their music to the very descriptive words that you may be wanting to use in your internet search.

## Intuitive Questions

*[see page 52: John Henry's Guidelines for Choosing the Best Music for Your Life]*

*Can you identify any artists or songs that you definitely DO resonate with?*

*Can you identify any artists or songs that you know you definitely DO NOT resonate with?*

*Can you think of any descriptive words to use in an internet search to discover new music that you might enjoy?*

**Suggested mantras in finding the best music for your life (feel free to tweak them to find what resonates best with you):**

*If my heart feels light, it's probably right!*

*I CAN find the music that is best for me!*

*I listen to music that feeds my soul, and I feel whole!*

# CHAPTER 6

# MUSIC AS MAGIC

This chapter is an invitation to your imagination. What is the appeal of a great fairytale or epic fantasy novel, if not the endless and fascinating interplay and battle between the forces of good and evil? In fairy tales and fantasies, the opposing forces of good and evil both wield magical powers, one force wielding light magic and the other dark magic.

This ongoing interplay between the forces of good and evil has persisted throughout millennia and still exists today, permeating much of our popular western culture. As a result, countless heroes, villains, and complex characters fill our favorite stories of epic myths, legends, and fantasies.

Let's take a look at some of the characteristics of both light and dark magic, as well as gray magic. I offer this alternative perspective as another barometer to gauge the Health of the music in your life. My intention in drawing a comparison between magic and music is to expand how we understand and discern the qualities of music on a sliding scale of dark to light energy. This can be done instead of, or in addition to, categorizing music on the spectrum of unHealthy to Healthy.

## Light Magic

Light magic seeks to embrace all in light and love. It brings diverse beings together in unity by illuminating everyone's common right to exist and enjoy life within the cosmos. Rather than seeking one-upmanship or rankings of superiority, it seeks teamwork, truth, compassion, and justice for all. Light magic is as impartial as the sun in its abundant giving of love, life, and protection to all in every direction.

*Do any fictional or real characters spring to mind for you that seem to embody light magic?*

## Dark Magic

Dark magic seeks to control, manipulate, force, coerce, deceive, destroy, disempower, create false hierarchies, divide, abuse, and otherwise bend reality to its own egotistical and perverse will.

*Do any fictional or real characters spring to mind for you that seem to embody dark magic?*

## Gray Magic

Like gray music, gray (or neutral) magic is a realm of magic that does not necessarily intend harm or benefit. Some gray magic is simply a weaker form of light magic that does indeed do a bit of good in the world, even if it's unintentional. Regardless, most gray magic tends to be self-oriented with little concern for the consequences. It may seek to gain an advantage over others, using questionable ethics, employing methods to confuse, bewilder, or mystify them. Gray magic may even creep into the darker realms by manipulating freedom of choice and personal will. While not completely devoid of the human heart, those who practice gray magic may not be overly concerned with lasting peace nor true justice for all.

*Do any fictional or real characters spring to mind for you that seem to embody gray magic?*

## Expanding Our Understanding of Music's Power

As we have discussed, music has tremendous power. When harnessed as light magic (intentional benefit to all), it can strengthen human bonds, deepen our self-awareness, and play a pivotal role in creating a peaceful world. It can remind us of our shared humanity and how much more similar we are than we might remember. However, when harnessed as dark magic (intentional harm to living beings), it can do the opposite and be a destructive force in our personal lives as well as our society and the environment at large.

The lion's share of the music that humans create

and consume in much of the world today emanates from a gray magic source. This type of music generally does not have a specific intention to either deeply harm or deeply benefit living beings. The danger, however, lies in our being only semi-conscious or unconscious of its influential power. When we fail to recognize the self-serving or sometimes shallow nature of this music, such a careless and unquestioned relationship to gray music can make us enablers allowing it to become a destructive force in society. If we don't consciously use music to enrich our world and promote peace, we may inadvertently allow it to work in the opposite way to degrade our planet and promote divisiveness.

I'd like to emphasize that the power of music is very much available to all people (not just musicians), especially in this digital age. For many of us, millions of songs lie waiting just a few button-presses away. So, what do we do once we've come to comprehend the various magical powers of music?

Marvel's much-loved web-slinging superhero Spider-Man is well-known for saying, "With great power comes great responsibility." Like any other form of power, it is critical to acknowledge the full extent of music's power, both negative and positive, so that we create, consume, and share it responsibly. Without our conscious awareness of its potentially harmful energies, we may unwittingly allow music to contribute to creating disharmony in our mind-body-spirit system, fracturing social connections, and influencing us to take a shallow and false view of ourselves and others. If you are familiar with the basic Spider-Man story, you may recall the part when he was more concerned with his external image than doing the right thing as a fatal incident unfolded. Spider-Man deeply regretted that he had allowed such a vain concern to overcome his better judgment and did not do all he could to prevent the fatality. Hopefully, we never have to face such extreme choices and circumstances, but it is a good metaphor that points to how forgetting our core values due to being distracted by something seemingly harmless can have significant and unintended consequences.

Since most of the music we are naturally exposed to is gray music, I encourage you to develop a regular habit of looking a little more closely at how music impacts and influences your life and its potential to influence others. From there, you will be more deeply empowered to co-create the world you would like to live in by making conscious music choices.

## Light Magic Music in Action

Music composed and imbued with the spirit of light magic can convey powerful and positive messages as well as support and champion a worthy cause. Allow me to share just a handful of examples that come to mind. The Paul McCartney song "Looking for Changes" advocates animal rights. The Angelique Kidjo song "Mother Nature" gives credence to the importance of listening to the voice of Mother Earth. The Bob Marley song "One Love" speaks about the power of uniting humanity through the omnipresent bond of love. I wrote a song in collaboration with Kenyan environmentalist Clifford Akwana "Let's Keep Our Water Clean," which addresses the important issue of water pollution. The Rock Asylum song "Being Different" speaks up against bullying. Def Tech's "ONGAKU" honors the incredible power of music. I can think of so many more, but I will stop here. Fortunately, there are countless such songs bringing messages of hope and inspiration to the world.

How many more worthy causes are out there that could benefit from having a few well-written pieces of music to help spread their life-affirming and dignifying message? Consider how powerful it would be if the vast majority of music produced and consumed were conscious music imbued with light magic highlighting our common humanity and our shared experience as inhabitants of planet Earth and the Universe!

## Sound Healing and Vibrational Awareness

Beyond heart-based inspirational pieces of music, sound healing is another expression of how music or thoughtfully composed soundscapes embody the realm of light magic. Through immersion in waves of specific sound frequencies and vibrations, the individual can be put into a state that promotes and accelerates healing on various levels of one's mind-body-spirit system. In some ways, it can be compared to taking a relaxing bath or receiving a healing massage. The healing power of sound is based on the concept that at a fundamental level, everything in the Universe is essentially vibration. When vibrations around us interact and intertwine in harmonious patterns, our body resonates with the harmonious frequencies, and it feels good. Because sound travels faster through water than through air, its calming and therapeutic effects are felt almost immediately in our bodies, which are composed mainly of water.

In recent years, there has become an increasing awareness about the benefits of tuning music to the frequencies of 432 Hz and 528 Hz,[19] which are said to be more aligned with the naturally occurring frequencies of the Earth and the cosmos, rather than our current standard of tuning which is 440 Hz. Each of the two naturally derived frequencies (432 Hz and 528 Hz) has its unique benefits to consider before choosing one over the other for tuning. While there is some debate over which is better, it is largely agreed that either one is more beneficial to our Health and well-being than the 440 Hz frequency used for tuning most music today.

Unlike frequencies attuned to natural resonance, 440 Hz[20] is not in harmony with the natural world,

---

19 Merriam Webster Dictionary defines Hertz as "A unit of frequency equal to one cycle per second – abbreviation Hz."
20 I feel I must mention that there are those who do not acknowledge any benefits to tuning music outside of 440 Hz. There have been several claims to debunk the benefits of 432 Hz and 528 Hz, citing

which makes it slightly dissonant in our bodies. So, when 440 Hz was adopted as the international tuning standard in the mid-20th century, some believe this was done intentionally to make it easier to control the human population by interfering with our natural state of harmony. As this unnatural frequency hinders deep levels of harmonic resonance in the individual, it engenders restlessness, agitation, and tension, which lends itself towards divisiveness and aggression. An old maxim of warfare is to "divide and conquer." Therefore, withdrawing the natural resonance frequencies and installing an unnatural frequency as the international standard would make controlling the human population that much easier. Whether you choose to believe this or not, it's a thought worth considering.

Since 440 Hz has been the international tuning standard for several decades, most of the music you and I are exposed to has been calibrated to this frequency. This does NOT mean that all music tuned to this frequency is bad for us; just that there may be a better alternative. For example, if a piece of light magic music is composed with the intention to heal, then that will come across regardless of the tuning frequency. However, research suggests that if such a piece of music is tuned to one of the universal frequencies such as 432

---

it as a fad to make money. Admittedly it may be difficult to actually "hear" the difference. All I know is that some of the most amazing sound healing journeys I have experienced have been tuned to 528 Hz!

Hz or 528 Hz, then the healing effect on a vibrational level could be even that much deeper.

Does this also apply to gray music? Yes. I firmly believe that the most crucial ingredient in a musical composition is the intention behind its creation. Since gray music is mostly created with a fairly neutral intent, it seems likely that converting it to 432 Hz or 528 Hz would deepen any positive attributes in the music. But would this also work for unHealthy music? Probably not since the toxic and harmful intentions behind the creation of dark magic music would likely outweigh any benefits from shifting the tuning frequency.

To understand the difference more fully between 440 Hz music versus 432 Hz and 528 Hz music, you could draw a rough comparison to what we eat. Non-organic fruits and vegetables would be like Healthy music tuned to 440 Hz. Organic fruits and vegetables would be like Healthy music tuned to either 432 Hz or 528 Hz. You could use your imagination to see how this could play out in the gray area foods, such as commercially manufactured white bread. As for unHealthy music, I am sure you would agree that there are no discernable Health benefits between consuming non-organic and organic narcotics and opioids; they both have substantial health risks regardless of the quality of the ingredients used to formulate these drugs.

As you travel along on your unique musical journey, I encourage you to consider how incorporating sound healing into your life[21] can perhaps be another wonderful and enjoyable tool to bring you a sense of greater well-being and joy. If you are interested in listening to music tuned to 432 Hz or 528 Hz and trying it out for yourself, a simple internet search for "music in 432 / 528 Hz" or "sound healing 432 / 528 Hz" will give you many options. In the resource section of this book, I have included recommended listening material and links to articles and videos about the 432 Hz and 528 Hz frequencies.

Music is such a precious resource and form of transmitting energy. I hope this chapter has further served to expand your ways of thinking around the magical powers of music and how we can, with a sense of responsibility, employ them to enrich our lives and our world.

---

*21 I've experienced great benefit from repeated immersion in the sound healing music of Lee Harris (www.LeeHarrisMusic.com). One of my favorite tracks for this purpose which I highly recommend is "All Who Walk the Earth – Lee Harris & Davor Bozic (Official Music Video) [528Hz Music]".*

## Intuitive Questions

*Do you have a sense of which music in your life might be imbued with light magic?*

*Is there any music in your life which you sense might be possessed by dark magic?*

*Do you feel that most of the music in your life contributes to your overall happiness, Health, and sense of being joyfully alive?*

*Do you feel that the music in your life is supporting your ever-expanding evolution as a human being?*

*Is there anything you could do in relation to music in your life to increase its beneficial impact and decrease its negative impact?*

*Do you consciously use sound healing in your own life? If not, how might you begin to incorporate some sound healing into your routine?*

# CONCLUSION

Thank you for accompanying me on this philosophical and practical journey about a subject that is very meaningful to me. If you made it this far, it's likely that you also share a passion for music and can recognize the impact, both positive and negative, that it can potentially have on your life. Has this book influenced your thinking around your musical choices in some helpful way? I hope so.

Your musical preferences and choices will evolve over time, so do not be afraid of becoming bored or getting stuck. There will always be new and exciting music out there to be explored. If you find that some of your current preferences in music are not as Healthy as they might be and you are not quite ready to give them up, please don't worry. My intention is only to shed light on the importance of knowing that we are sensitive vibrational beings who are influenced by the sound vibrations in the world around us.

When you surround yourself and others with healing and empowering sound vibrations, your own positive energy field and your natural ability to influence your environment positively will increase. As you begin to experience more of this in your own life, your less-empowering choices will gradually and naturally evolve into different, more empowering, and beneficial ones.

My cherished hope is to live in and co-create a world where people are empowered daily to create greater Health for themselves at every level. Let's use music to help make our personal world and the world at large a brighter, lighter, and more joyful place than any of us can even now imagine! It's up to us.

Will you take this message and apply it in your own life to create greater Health for yourself? Ultimately, the choice is yours.

And as I say farewell, for now, I am sending you wishes for an abundance of Health, joy, and prosperity, as well as countless moments of musical enrichment ahead!

# APPENDIX

# APPENDIX A

## Ten Ways to Enrich Your Life With Music

In this section, I cover a handful of ideas that you can use to enrich your life with music. Some ideas may be new for you, some may not, and maybe some ideas you have just not thought about in a while. Perhaps you could think of several additional Healthy ways of your own in which you currently use music in your life already.

I present the following ten ways in the hopes that some of them will resonate with you and inspire you to take a fresh look at the role music plays in your life going forward.

Please peruse the suggestions below as simply ideas to play with and entertain briefly. If something strikes a chord (pun intended!) with you and you are moved to take inspired action, please do so allowing your own inner wisdom and intelligence to guide you as to the appropriate steps for *your* personal journey. I encourage you to take it all in very lightly. There is no "should" or pressure that I care to exert on you or anyone. I simply feel called to share various possibilities as they relate to the subject matter of the book and to potentially expand your frame of reference as to possible ways to enhance your life through the conscious and mindful bringing in of musical elements.

## 1. Create your own "Inspirational Music Playlist"

Whether your music is on your computer, your portable music player, or if you have an old school CD player, I recommend putting a bunch of your favorite songs, tracks, and musical compositions together in one place. If your musical collection is digital, you can create a playlist. If you are using an "old-fashioned" stereo system to listen to music, you may elect to either burn a CD of your favorite tunes or put a bunch of your favorite albums in a neat pile near your stereo system.

The next step is to *listen to this music.* When feasible, anytime, anywhere, and often. Especially when you are not feeling in such a great mood, put on your "Inspirational Music Playlist". Put on those tunes that inspire you, that uplift you, that remind you why you are glad to be alive. Listen to the ones that remind you of your dreams and bring you back to your center, to the present moment and help you to remember to see everything in your life as magical and meaningful.

Only *you* know all those songs that you really love. Find them, put them on this list and listen to them often. You can create a great tool like this to have at your disposal to boost your spirits and help you to feel better when you need to.

## 2. Walk, jog, or sit outdoors with some of your favorite upbeat tunes

Walking can be a wonderful leisurely and Healthy way to pass the time. For walking I personally find that the listening choices can be of a wide variety since walking is basically relaxing and generally does not require as much focus or energy as jogging for example. Perhaps try some relaxing music for a leisurely stroll, or mid to up-tempo songs could work well for a quick-paced walk.

Jogging is a good way to energize and strengthen the body if you seek something more vigorous than a brisk walk. As a jogger I find that having good songs on my personal music player is quite helpful for me to be inspired to get out there and have a good run. From experience I know that when I listen to slow and dreary songs, it generally does not produce inspiring results in my running experience. On the other hand, when I have upbeat and energetic, moderate to up-tempo tunes to listen to, my run generally feels good, and I tend to have increased motivation to do the run.

Sometimes you may not feel like walking or jogging (or may not have the inclination or the capacity to do so). When this is the case, I wonder if you might explore the possibility of spending time out of doors listening to the music of your choice. There is nothing quite like fresh air and an open sky to help bring us into the present moment and remind us of the bigger picture that we are all participating in and cocreating together.

## 3. Listen to relaxing music at a low volume during dinner time (or any appropriate mealtime)

Well-selected relaxing music can be used to settle down the mood of a room and encourage us to eat slower and mindfully. In our fast-paced, rush-rush society it can be very hard to eat food slowly and to be mindful enough not to distract ourselves with other things (such as an electronic device, the TV, or printed material) while we are eating. Why not try to slow down for at least one meal per day (when possible), to bring presence and appreciation to the food we are eating, to oneself, and to the people we may be in the company of? This can be applied whether eating alone or with others.

Slower, relaxed eating is not only more enjoyable and calming, but it also may encourage us to eat less food yet feel a deeper sense of satisfaction than we might if we felt stressed and hurried. It can also bring you into the present moment and enables you to step out of your head for a period in your day.

If you are eating in a group environment, quiet and relaxing music may help to engender an atmosphere of talking and peacefully communicating with one another. Historically, in many cultures around the world, mealtime has been a traditional coming together of the family and community members. It helps remind us of our common humanity, that we need each other, and that we are not so different from each other after all.

## 4. Give 15-30 minutes to yourself at night or in the morning to lie down and do some gentle stretching to the backdrop of relaxing music

While lying down, you can do some gentle yoga if you know some simple poses for relaxation. If you are not familiar with yoga, you can simply try lying on your back on the floor. Please use a mat or lie on a rug or even a bed (a bare hard wood or stone floor may not work well).

While lying flat on your back, begin focusing on deepening your breath. Legs near each other but not touching, let your arms and feet flop out to the side if you have room. That's really all there is to it. As you do so, you may have the desire to bring your knees to your chest and lightly hold onto them. In this position you might try to rock gently from side to side as you deepen both your listening and breathing.

The only objective here is to feel good and return to that carefree state of a child. You can use this precious time to relax deeply while enjoying the inner journey that the music will bring you on. You may feel better, a deeper sense of relaxation and more balance.

It's not so hard to find good music for this purpose. You can search the internet or your favorite music streaming platform. Just type in something like "relaxing music", "gentle music", "music for meditation" or "New-age music" and see what pops up. From there you can do some exploring and find out what type of music you are attracted to most for this purpose. YouTube can be great for accessing various music easily and much of it for free.

## 5. Take music lessons

This applies to people of all ages – really! Even people who are well-advanced in years or who have physical or mental limitations can benefit from learning about music through lessons.

Taking music lessons in and of itself has many inherent and simple benefits that can help anyone. It can be fun and exciting to learn a new instrument or simply to learn *about* music. A basic music theory or music history class could generate a deeper appreciation and therefore enjoyment of music in your life.

There is no need to try to become the next Wolfgang Amadeus Mozart nor Jimi Hendrix. Taking music lessons has nothing to do with comparing yourself to other people. However, should you be so inclined, taking music lessons to truly become a proficient player has its own abundance of beneficial points. Some of the benefits of learning to play an instrument deeply are the following: learning to be expressive, learning to read music (which is effectively another language), understanding how musical notes relate to each other in time and space (which can help us deepen our grasp of science and mathematical concepts among other things), experiencing the rewards of a student-teacher relationship, sharing your performances with others, learning how to listen deeply and so many more benefits.

Even if you only end up learning the names of 3 notes, you are still learning something new which will create new connections and pathways in your brain helping to keep your brain young. There is much to be said about simply enjoying the process of learning something new. It can be refreshing and engaging and simply put, fun! Don't worry about how far you're going to get. Just start if you are so inspired.

## 6. Dance as is appropriate for your body

Seems simple enough right? Basically, the main idea is to incorporate dancing or moving your body rhythmically more often into your daily routine. If you're the type of person who would be more likely to be motivated to get up and dance in a formal setting such as a class, then perhaps you may enjoy joining a local dance class. If, however you have no qualms about getting down and boogying right in the privacy of your own home, then that's what I'm talking about as well.

Dancing makes us feel better. Our bodies like to move and when they are in the habit of moving it's easier to continue moving, but when we lose the habit of moving on a regular basis it becomes very easy to not want to move around much at all. Dancing is a fun and fairly simple way to get moving. It doesn't have to be fancy, just swaying from side to side can be nice. Music is the engine that propels our body in this case. We can use it to our advantage to be more physically active.

Dancing heals us as it reminds us of the joy of living and the importance of taking advantage of the present moment. If you have physical limitations or bodily pains that make dancing impractical for you, you can still perhaps sway back in forth in your chair or bob your head up and down or come up with some other creative way that *you* can think of. Put on your favorite song and make it "Groove-Out Time"!

If you *can* dance with friends or family members whether it be at home, at a party or in another setting, that could be fantastic. Dancing makes us feel good and connects us with the rhythm of life.

And let me emphasize that it need not be any particular way. I am not talking about performing a dance that gets rated by judges as to its perfection of form. Actually, I would suggest the goofier the better. The more you just allow your body to move and groove without judging it, the more of your natural energy will be allowed to flow freely which may in turn release energy blocks and allow for more flow in your life in general.

## 7. Sing!

This is such a simple and perhaps overlooked daily practice that is available to most people all the time. You don't have to sing loudly, in front of others, or even in key! It doesn't matter if you are a "good singer" or not. Of course, when doing anything that can have an effect on others, we want to take into consideration our neighbors, family members and other people besides just ourselves. While probably nobody appreciates when someone is disturbing their peace, I am still sure that even if you are not surrounded by your biggest fans, you can find a short moment or two throughout the day to sing or hum a little something quietly to yourself!

Maybe the shower is the safest place for you. Maybe in the car by yourself or perhaps you have a park nearby that you can take a walk in when it is not crowded. There are many creative ways to go about this if you do not feel comfortable simply singing at home.

And if you *do* love to sing and if those whom you live with do not mind it, then please do sing at home to your heart's content. Sing for others if you are moved to do so. It can be a beautiful gift when shared from the heart with consideration.

Some people may prefer to hum or whistle. This can be a great way to pass the time in some circumstances. Whistling is also a form of singing in my opinion. When we hear a birdsong, we regard it as singing (the word "song" and "sing" are etymologically connected) even though it often sounds more like a whistle right?

Just vocalize music in some way and don't worry about how "amateur" it is. If *you* enjoy it, that will carry through and *you'll* feel better which will be an inspiration to others. It will also have the effect of uplifting your own mood and, in this way, you will bring an uplifted presence to those in your sphere of influence.

## 8. Purge your music library

OK I know. This one is kind of strict, but I'm serious about this. It was a very beneficial process that I underwent in my own life and that I still undergo from time to time to keep things fresh. As a youth I was a huge music collector. I had many cassette tapes and CDs.

Eventually I threw out the albums that over time I had come to sense were basically negative in vibration for me. While it took some determination, I felt better! Since the purging of my music collection years ago (around 2008) I have barely missed any of the music that I have parted with. From time to time there would pop up a song or an artist that I would be in the mood to listen to but couldn't. However, the feeling would quickly pass. I never regretted my choice to purge my music library.

What happens after the process of purging can be challenging but it is also fun and exciting. That is, building up a new collection of music slowly over time. For me it was challenging because I was in my late 20's, living on my own and no longer had the money to spend on leisure time as I did when I was a teenager. Additionally, the music landscape was changing drastically as CD's and tapes were long falling out of fashion. I wasn't sure how to go about finding and obtaining new music in this changed environment. I listened to my heart however and over time have come to have a new collection of music that I now use and incorporate into my life much more consciously and enjoy in a much Healthier way than I did before.

Being open to new music as I was, I even attracted many CD's and vinyl records given to me for free by others who were ready to part with them. I then underwent a purging process over time with these newly acquired albums as well (often through giving away or in a yard sale) since not all were a good fit for the music that I wanted in my life. I also learned that not *all* "Healthy" music was a good fit for my life. It was up to me to find the Healthy music that was a match for me and my lifestyle.

Getting rid of all the stuff in my music collection that was no longer serving me really helped me to feel lighter, and to feel cleansed in my heart, mind and even my body! So, I simply recommend, (whether it be digital collections, CD's, vinyl records, or cassette tapes) to get rid of any music that you truly know is no longer serving you in a Healthy way. Also, I strongly suggest you throw the truly negative stuff away in the trash bin (either physical or digital). Don't just give it away. If you truly sense that there is an overall negative vibration to the music, then chances are that negativity will also contaminate the energy field of the next person.

If you judge the album to be good quality gray music and you do not feel so strongly about its negative energy being a problem in your life, then that might be something to consider giving away or selling. I would like to point out: when we clear our environment of negative energy it benefits everybody. If we just pass along the negative energy to our neighbor, it still lingers in our environment.

## 9. Attend local concerts or musical events (either in-person or online)

Enjoying live music performances can be a truly exhilarating experience. There is stuff going on everywhere around the world musically. If you can find a good local concert or event to attend from time to time, it may uplift your spirits (especially if you choose a good one). Perhaps try to attend shows with an artist, genre, or cause that you really care about so you can set yourself up for a very enjoyable time.

When we consciously choose to socialize with other people, maybe dance, maybe sing along, maybe chat with others, maybe just sit and enjoy being entertained as part of the audience, we are having a social impact and can contribute to our environment in a beneficial way. And when we are making a positive contribution to our environment, we are also making a difference in our own life as well as the lives of others. Social, and musical events tend to really give us a chance to simply relax and be a regular human being, which can be hard to do in our fast-paced, hyper self-conscious, and judgmental society.

## 10. Carefully choose the soundtrack to your daily life and activities

While this suggestion is similar to #1 on this list, the emphasis here is on assisting your productivity and bringing your best self forward in your work, chores and studies rather than just focusing on listening to your favorite inspirational tunes. If, for example, you are commuting to work or school with a gangsta rap song or a death metal song blasting in your ears, chances are you may forget to greet the first few people you meet with an enthusiastic smile and a friendly "How are you?". You might be the rare exception who *can* do that, but even still I would bet that your body chemistry would be a bit too wired to bring a truly relaxed heart into your environment.

When I travel and listen to even light rock music, I still notice that I may become a bit more energized than the situation I'm heading into may call for. I then find that I must pull myself out of that energetically exaggerated state and back to my calm center so that I can be fully present to engage in the thoughtful energetic exchanges that I prefer to conduct with the people in my life. Should I want to truly communicate with someone in a Healthy, open, and compassionate way, it is important for me to maintain a purity of my own consciousness.

If you are working at a desk and are allowed to listen to music of your own choosing, why not choose music that will really enable you to concentrate, to feel relaxed, and to zone in on the work you are doing? Whenever I listen to very active music, and especially if the vocals are prominent, I can't get anything done without feeling like half my mind is somewhere else!

Be wary of listening to music that is too distracting or energy-robbing. This type of music can have a negative impact on your life, your environment, and your results at work.

I am aware that each person is unique, but I imagine there is a commonality amongst most of us as to the benefit of choosing the most appropriate music for our environment. Choose the music that you respond to best while in your productive mode, not necessarily your favorite music. It may take some trial and error, but I believe you will be glad you did.

Choosing the best music for our work (whether it be schoolwork, professional work, or personal work) environment can help to keep us calm, centered, zoned-in and productive.

I truly hope that you can extract some value from reviewing the suggestions above and that you feel further empowered as to how you can enrich your life with music in real and practical ways. As a popular adage goes "Be the change you wish to see in the world". Your example of enriching your own life with music can inspire others to do the same.

# APPENDIX B

## John Henry's Recommended Listening List

    This is a selection of some of the music that I have found, over the course of my music listening life, to be enjoyable and inspirational to listen to. I have tried to include multiple genres for variety. I understand these artists are suited to my tastes and may seem limited to you in scope. My music library is always evolving however, and I am open to listen to anything that catches my fancy.

    As I've talked about in the book, most music available for public consumption in the world today is gray music. Of the genres I include below, I readily consider the following as gray music (containing both Healthy and unHealthy aspects) and to be approached with that awareness: Hard Rock, Heavy Metal, Rock, Pop, Singer-Songwriter, Folk, Reggae, Hip Hop, Rap, Country, and Independent. I always try to filter through and choose the most positive and enjoyable songs from these genres which can take some trial and error. Those that I include below I feel are somewhere on the mid to light gray Healthier end of the gray area spectrum. The genres that I feel comfortable to broadly regard as mostly light gray to Healthy would be New-Age, Worldbeat, Ambient, Sound Healing, Fusion, Instrumental, Jazz,

World, and Classical (Western).

Please approach the recommended list of music below using your own good sense.[22] What may be uplifting for one person may have a very different effect on someone else. Of course, there's no need for you to enjoy the same music as me, but I offer these for your consideration and hope that you may find some clues as to what lights you up musically.

Many artists can fit into more than one genre. For ease of listing artists according to recognizable tastes I approached each genre in a very broad sense and have grouped several together in some cases. So, forgive me if you feel that my categories are a bit oversimplified.

These are just some of the artists that I have enjoyed listening to. There are so many more, but I wanted to end this book with at least some suggestions to hopefully expose you to some music you may not be familiar with or perhaps that you may have forgotten that you liked.

---

22 *A note of caution as to children and sensitive people in your environment: I suggest exploring any gray music recommendations by yourself at first. Then, if the music is in accord with your own personal standards, you will feel empowered to know as to whom you might appropriately share it with. For example, there is some hard rock and heavy metal music that I feel happy to share with my young son. However, I am selective as to which songs I choose to expose him to as well as how much and the time of day. While playing 10 carefully selected heavy metal songs to my child right before bed may not be Healthy, playing maybe 2 or 3 in the middle of the afternoon to enjoy and move some energy around might be perfectly fine.*

## John Henry's Recommended Listening List

I do include specific album or song recommendations for many artists listed below though not in all cases. Perhaps a good way to begin is to start with a genre that might interest you. The albums and songs I've included under any artist are just a suggested entry point into that artist for further exploration. This list is by no means exhaustive, but I hope it provides some trailheads for your musical adventures up ahead. Try searching any of the music on this list.

I am sending you much love, light, laughter, and a wish for you to rekindle your passion for music ever deeper in your life for the benefit of your Health and the well-being of all!!!

Happy exploring!

To download a PDF of "John Henry's Recommended Listening List" with hyperlinks visit:

https://johnhenrysheridanmusic.com/mind-your-music-book

## New-Age / Worldbeat / Ambient / Sound Healing (432 / 528 Hz)

**Andreas Vollenweider & Friends** (Switzerland - Zürich)
*Down to the Moon* - [album]
*White Winds (Seeker's Journey)* – [album]
*Dancing with the Lion* – [album]

**Awakening Planet** (Norway)

**Brulé** (U.S.A. – Lower Brule, SD)
*Star People* – [album]

**David Arkenstone** – (U.S.A.)

**Enigma** (Germany)
*MCMXC A.D.* – [album]
*Cross of Changes* - [album]

**Infinite Waters (Diving Deep) / Music** (U.K. / U.S.A.)
"432 Hz DNA Healing/ Chakra Cleansing Meditation/Relaxation Music"
"432 Hz | DNA Repair | Powerful Third Eye Opening Binaural Beat | Relaxation Sleep Music – 7 Chakras"
"528 Hz | Healing Sounds (1 Hour) Meditation – Calming & Relaxing"

**Kailash Kokopelli** (Earth)
*Sakrayaami: Didgeridoo Trance Formations* – [album]

**Kitaro** (Japan - Aichi)

**Lee Harris** (U.K. / U.S.A.)
*Awaken (528Hz)* – [album]
*All Who Walk the Earth (528Hz)*– [single]

**Meditation and Healing** (U.K.)
"528 Hz Miracle Healing Music | Let Go of Negative Energy | Deep Healing Music for the Body & Soul"

**Patrick O'Hearn** (U.S.A. – Los Angeles, CA)
*Trust* – [album]
*Metaphor* – [album]

**Yanni** (Greece / U.S.A.)
*Devotion (The Best of Yanni)* – [album]
*Live at the Acropolis* – [album]

## Instrumental / Fusion / Jazz / World

**Alip_Ba_Ta** – (Indonesia)
"Another Day [Dream Theater Cover]" – [single]

**D'Gary** (Madagascar)

**Herbie Hancock** (U.S.A.)

## John Henry's Recommended Listening List

**Jake Shimabukuro**
(U.S.A. – Hawaii)

**Joe Robinson**
(Australia / U.S.A.)

**Lee Ritenour**
(U.S.A. – Los Angeles, CA)

**Miroslav Tadić** (Serbia)

**Piotr Restecki** (Poland)

**Ravi Shankar** – (India)
*Passages (Ravi Shankar and Phillip Glass)* – [album]

**Wayne Shorter** (U.S.A.)

## Classical (Western)

**Antonín Dvořák**
(Czech Republic)

**Agustín Barrios**
(Paraguay)

**Edvard Grieg** (Norway)

**Erik Satie** (France)

**Frédéric Chopin** (Poland)

**Georg Friedrich Händel**
(Germany / U.K.)

**Gustav Mahler** (Austria)

**Gustav Holst** (U.K.)

**Heitor Villa-Lobos** (Cuba)

**Jean Sibelius** (Finland)

**Johan Sebastian Bach**
(Germany)

**Johannes Brahms**
(Germany)

**Léo Brouwer**
(Cuba / U.S.A.)

**Ludwig Van Beethoven**
(Germany)

**Pyotr Ilyich Tchaikovsky**
(Russia)

**Wolfgang Amadeus Mozart**
(Austria / Germany)

## Hard Rock / Heavy Metal

**AC/DC**
(Australia - Sydney)
*Back in Black* - [album]
*Live* - [album]
*Let There Be Rock* – [album]

**Amorphis**
(Finland - Helsinki)
*Tales from the Thousand Lakes* – [album]
*Elegy* – [album]
*"Black Winter Day"* – [single]
*"My Kantele"* – [single]

**Black Sabbath**
(U.K. – Birmingham)
*"After Forever"* – [single]
*"Never Say Die"* – [single]

**Def Leppard**
(U.K. - Sheffield)

Hysteria – [album]
Adrenalize – [album]

**Dream Theater**
(U.S.A. – Boston, MA)
Awake – [album]
"Another Day" – [single]
"Space-Dye Vest" – [single]

**Helloween**
(Germany – Hamburg)
Keeper of the Seven Keys, Pts. I & II (Deluxe Edition) – [album]
"A Little Time" – [single]
"Perfect Gentleman" – [single]
"If I Could Fly" – [single]

**Iron Maiden**
(U.K. - London)
Piece of Mind – [album]
Somewhere in Time - [album]

**Joe Satriani** (U.S.A.)
Is There Love in Space? – [album]
Super Colossal – [album]

**Metallica**
(U.S.A. - California)
"Fade to Black" – [single]
"For Whom the Bell Tolls" – [single]

**Omnium Gatherum**
(Finland - Karhula)
The Burning Cold – [album]
"Refining Fire" – [single]
"Be the Sky" – [single]

**Savatage**
(U.S.A. – Florida)
Edge of Thorns – [album]
"Summer's Rain" – [single]

**Van Halen**
(U.S.A. – California)
1984 – [album]
For Unlawful Carnal Knowledge – [album]
"Dreams" – [single]
"Right Now" – [single]

**ZO2**
(U.S.A. – Brooklyn, NY)
"Ain't It Beautiful" – [single]
"I Will Be Alright" – [single]

# Pop / Singer-Songwriter / Folk / Rock / Reggae / World

**Aerosmith**
(U.S.A – Boston, MA)
"Dream On" – [single]
"Nobody's Fault" – [single]

**Alanis Morissette**
(Canada – Ottawa, ON / U.S.A.)
"You Learn" – [single]
"Thank U" – [single]

**Anathema**
(U.K. - Liverpool)
"Untouchable (part one)" – [single]

## John Henry's Recommended Listening List

**Andrea Bocelli** (Italy)
*Romanza (20th Anniversary Edition / Deluxe)* – [album]
"*Con Te Partirò*" – [single]

**Angelique Kidjo** (Benin)
"*Mother Nature (ft. Sting)*" – [single]

**B-52's**
(U.S.A. – Athens, GA)
*Cosmic Thing* – [album]
"*Roam*" – [single]

**Barry Manilow**
(U.S.A. – Brooklyn, NY)
*Even Now* – [album]

**Beatles, The**
(U.K. - Liverpool)

**Billy Joel**
(U.S.A. – New York City, NY)
*Storm Front* – [album]
*Glass Houses* – [album]
*52nd Street* – [album]
"*And So It Goes*" – [single]

**Bob Dylan** (U.S.A.)
Bob Marley (Jamaica)
"*One Love / People Get Ready*" – [single]

**Céline Dion**
(Canada - Quebec)
"*I'm Alive*" – [single]
"*A New Day Has Come*" – [single]

**Coldplay** (U.K. - London)
"*Clocks*" – [single]

**Cranberries, The**
(Ireland - Limerick)
"*Linger*" – [single]

"*Dreams*" – [single]

**Creedence Clearwater Revival** (El Cerrito, CA)
"*Have You Ever Seen the Rain*" – [single]
"*Lookin' Out My Back Door*" – [single]

**Cure, The**
(U.K. – West Sussex)
"*Fascination Street*" – [single]
"*Friday I'm In Love*" – [single]

**Cyndi Lauper**
(U.S.A. – New York City, NY)
*She's So Unusual* – [album]
*True Colors* – [album]
"*Change of Heart*" – [single]
"*True Colors*" – [single]

**Dido** (U.K. – London)
*Safe Trip Home* – [album]
"*White Flag (Acoustic)*" – [single]

**Elton John** (U.K.)
*The One* – [album]
"*Rocket Man*" – [single]

**Engenheiros do Hawaii**
(Brazil – Porto Alegre)
"*Até O Fim (Ao Vivo)*" – [single]
"*Infinita Highway (Ao Vivo)*" – [single]

**Genesis** (U.K. – Surrey)
*We Can't Dance* – [album]
"*No Son of Mine*" – [single]

**Guns N' Roses**
(U.S.A. – Los Angeles, CA)
"Patience" – [single]
"November Rain" – [single]
"Estranged" – [single]
"Sweet Child O' Mine" - [single]

**Howard Jones**
(U.K. - London)
Cross That Line – [album]
In the Running – [album]
"The Prisoner" – [single]
"Lift Me Up" – [single]

**Jackson Browne** (U.S.A. – Los Angeles, CA)
"Take It Easy" – [single]
"These Days" – [single]

**James Taylor** (U.S.A.)
"Carolina in My Mind (from Pull Over)" – [single]
"Fire & Rain" – [single]
"Sweet Baby James" – [single]

**Jeff Beck** (U.K.)
"Cause We've Ended as Lovers" – [single]
"Nadia" – [single]
"Roy's Toy" – [single]

**Jim Croce**
(U.S.A. – Philadelphia, PA)
Photographs & Memories: His Greatest Hits – [album]
"Lover's Cross" – [single]
"I Got a Name" – [single]

**Jimi Hendrix** (U.S.A.)
"All Along the Watchtower" – [single]

**John Denver** (U.S.A.)
"Take Me Home, Country Roads" – [single]

**John Fogerty**
(U.S.A. – El Cerrito, CA)
"Centerfield" – [single]

**Kazuya Yoshii**
(Japan - Tokyo)
"Weekender" – [single]
"ビルマニア (Biru Mania)" – [single]

**Kenna** (Ethiopia / U.S.A.)
"Hell Bent" – [single]

**Kyū Sakamoto**
(Japan - Kanagawa)
"Sukiyaki" – [single]
"Miagete Goran Yoru No Hoshi Wo" – [single]

**Legião Urbana** (Brazil – Brasília, Distrito Federal)
"Pais E Filhos" – [single]
"Eu Sei" – [single]

**Macka B** (U.K. / Jamaica)
"Wha Me Eat" – [single]
"Don't Give Up" – [single]

**Marc Anthony**
(U.S.A. – New York City, NY)
"Vivir Mi Vida" – [single]

**Moody Blues, The**
(U.K. – Birmingham)
"Your Wildest Dreams" – [single]
"I Know You're Out There Somewhere" – [single]

## John Henry's Recommended Listening List

**Natalie Imbruglia**
(Australia - Sydney)
*"Torn" – [single]*

**Pearl Jam**
(U.S.A. - Seattle)
*"Alive" – [single]*
*"Evenflow" – [single]*

**Phil Collins**
(U.K. - Middlesex)
*"In the Air Tonight" – [single]*
*"Another Day in Paradise" – [single]*

**Red Hot Chili Peppers**
(U.S.A. – Los Angeles, CA)
*"Dani California" – [single]*
*"Snow (Hey Oh)" – [single]*
*"Under the Bridge" – [single]*

**R.E.M.**
(U.S.A. – Athens, GA)
*"The One I Love" – [single]*

**Sade** (Nigeria / U.K.)
*Love Deluxe – [album]*
*"No Ordinary Love" – [single]*
*"Cherish the Day" – [single]*

**Sarah McLachlan** (Canada – Halifax, Nova Scotia)
*Fumbling Towards Ecstasy – [album]*
*Surfacing – [album]*
*"Angel" – [single]*
*"Sweet Surrender" – [single]*

**Seal** (U.K. - London)
*Seal – [album]*
*Seal II – [album]*
*"Crazy" – [single]*
*"Kiss from a Rose" – [single]*

**Simon & Garfunkel**
(U.S.A. – Queens, NY)
*Sounds of Silence – [album]*
*Parsley, Sage, Rosemary and Thyme – [album]*
*"I Am a Rock" – [single]*
*"The 59$^{th}$ Street Bridge Song" – [single]*

**Smashing Pumpkins**
(U.S.A. – Chicago, IL)
*"Raindrops + Sunshowers" – [single]*
*"With Every Light" – [single]*
*"Tonight, Tonight" – [single]*

**Stevie Ray Vaughn**
(U.S.A. – Austin, TX)
*Couldn't Stand the Weather (Legacy Edition) – [album]*
*"Little Wing" – [single]*

**Sting** (U.K.)
*Ten Summoner's Tales – [album]*
*Brand New Day – [album]*
*"Desert Rose" – [single]*
*"Shape of My Heart" – [single]*

**Tina Turner** (U.S.A.)
*"What's Love Got to Do with It" – [single]*

**Tom Petty**
(U.S.A. – Gainesville, FL)
"Runnin' Down a Dream" – [single]
"Learning To Fly (Version 1)" – [single]

**UB40** (U.K. - Birmingham)
"Cherry Oh Baby" – [single]

**U2** (Ireland - Dublin)
"I Still Haven't Found What I'm Looking For" – [single]
"A Beautiful Day" – [single]

**Youssou N'Dour**
(Senegal)
Joko: The Link – [album]
The Guide (Wommat) – [album]

**Zé Ramalho**
(Brazil - Paraíba)
"Batendo na Porta do Céu (Knockin' on Heaven's Door)" – [single]

## Country

**Charley Pride**
(U.S.A. – the South)
"Roll On Mississippi" – [single]

**The Highwaymen**
(U.S.A.)
Highwayman 2 – [album]
"Silver Stallion" – [single]

**Kenny Rogers**
(U.S.A. – the South)

**Willie Nelson**
(U.S.A. – TX)
"On the Road Again" – [single]

## Hip Hop / Rap

**Boyz II Men**
(U.S.A. – Philadelphia, PA)
"Motownphilly" – [single]

**Def Tech**
(Japan / U.S.A. - Hawaii)
"Golden Age" – [single]

**2Pac** (U.S.A.)
"Dear Mama" – [single]

## Independent (Various Genres)

**Ben Brinton**
(U.S.A. - Utah)
Pocket Octavez – [album]
"Polka Dot Mercy" – [single]

**Broccoli King, The**
(U.K. - Cambridge)
"I Can Be Your Friend" – [single]
"Don't Take It Out on Me" – [single]

**Chimeido** (Japan - Hyōgo)
"Umareru Tsubomi" – [single]
"New Beginnings" – [single]

## John Henry's Recommended Listening List

**Chris Robley**
(U.S.A. - Maine)
"Irretrievable Beauty" – [single]
"Collapsing Star" – [single]
"1+1+1=3" – [single]

**John Henry Sheridan**
(U.S.A. – Brooklyn, NY)
Cornucopia – [album]
"Daddy" – [single]
"Marching Marshmallows" – [single]
"Eagle Fly Free" – [single]

**Kimaguren** (Japan)
"Life" – [single]

**Lunatrek** (U.S.A.)
"Eclipse" – [single]
"Bubblespace" – [single]

**Marco Varisco**
(U.S.A. – Brooklyn, NY)
"Crash My Car" – [single]
"2nd Time Around" – [single]

**Maria Neckam** (Austria / U.S.A. – Brooklyn, NY)
"Familiar" – [single]

**Mike Bankhead**
(U.S.A. - Ohio)
"Wapakoneta" – [single]

**Nemo Re** (**Nemanja Rebic**) (Serbia / U.S.A.)
"High Abode" – [single]
"Mila" – [single]

**Paulie Z** (U.S.A.)
"Rise Again" – [single]
"A Call to Love" – [single]

**Smalltown Poets** (U.S.A.)
"Love Is the Ocean" – [single]

**Stolen Silver** (U.S.A.)
"Awake and Alive" – [single]
"Prefontaine" – [single]

**Tyrants in Therapy**
(U.S.A. - Los Angeles, CA)
"Too Tough to Cry" – [single]

# APPENDIX C

## Additional Resources

The resources I've provided below are merely entry points into further exploration for you to consider while pondering the ideas presented in this book. For most of them I have only skimmed through to see that they further elucidate the principles I have been speaking of. I believe you may find some helpful and eye-opening information below. The journey continues.

To download a PDF of "Additional Resources" with hyperlinks visit:

https://johnhenrysheridanmusic.com/mind-your-music-book

**Preface**

[ARTICLE] "The Benefits of Minimalism: 7 Reasons to Declutter Your Life" from Tiny Buddha website by Mel Johnson

[VIDEO] "Top 10 Things to Declutter Right Now" – from Joshua Becker YouTube Channel (August 28, 2020)

Additional Resources

## Chapter 1 – Beautiful Music and Vibrant Health Are Harmonious

*Is There a Link Between Music and Health?*
(see resources listed for Chapter 3)

## Chapter 2 – Why is the Mind Your Music Conversation Relevant?

*Advantages and Disadvantages of Technology*
[VIDEO] "The Pros and Cons of Technology with Jared Leto and Walter Isaacson" from RYOT YouTube Channel (July 20, 2017)

*Profit and "Progress" Over People*
[VIDEO] "Should We Put People Over Profit?" from Graham Cochrane YouTube Channel (October 15, 2019)

*We Are What We Consume*
[ARTICLE] "Popular Culture: We Are What We Consume" from Psychology Today website by Jim Taylor Ph.D (December 8, 2009)
[VIDEO] "You are what you CONSUME" from Coach PJ Nestler YouTube Channel (June 6, 2019)

*Proactive Rather Than Reactive*
[ARTICLE] "Proactive vs reactive thinking" from Proactive Mindfulness website
[VIDEO] "What is Proactivity? | Proactive vs Reactive" from Alberto Nodale YouTube Channel (February 3, 2020)

## Chapter 3 – Music Can Enrich Our Lives

*Rethinking the Role and Value of Music*

[ARTICLE] "20 Surprising, Science-Backed Health Benefits of Music" from Greatist website by Scott Christ (December 12, 2013)

[ARTICLE] "5 Ways Music Improves Our Health" from Huffington Post website by Jill Suttie (February 02, 2015)

[ARTICLE] "Music Therapy Could Ease Anxiety in Patients with Respiratory Failure, Study Finds" from Huffington Post website (May 20, 2013)

[ARTICLE] "Music Therapy for Health and Wellness" from Psychology Today website by Catherine Ulbricht Pharm. D. (June 21, 2013)

[VIDEO] "Top 10 Amazing Proven Health Benefits of Music - TopTenzNet" from TopTenz YouTube Channel (September 28, 2015)

[VIDEO] "The Benefits of Music Education - Riff Academy Homeschool Music Curriculum" from Riff Academy: Music Made Easy (November 4, 2013)

[VIDEO] "The Positive Psychological Effects of Music – Benefits of Making and Listening to Music" from Practical Psychology YouTube Channel (January 12, 2017)

Additional Resources

## Chapter 4 – The Sliding Scale of UnHealthy to Healthy Music

*UnHealthy Music / Gray Music*

[ARTICLE] "10 Surprising Ways Music Can Be Bad For You" from ListVerse website by Mike Floorwalker (June 25, 2016)

[ARTICLE] "'Healthy' and 'Unhealthy' Songs: Boston Commission's Top 10" from WBUR website by Carey Goldberg (December 21, 2010)

*Healthy Music*

(see resources listed in Chapter 3)

## Chapter 5 – How Can You Find the Best Music for You?

*Sorting it All Out*

[VIDEO] "'I AM what I CHOOSE to become' – Carl Jung Wisdom" from Team Fearless YouTube Channel (February 3, 2021)

[VIDEO] "How to Develop Your Intuition: A Simple Step by Step Process" from Aaron Doughty YouTube Channel (October 28, 2016)

## Chapter 6 – Music as Magic

*Light Magic*

[VIDEO] "Marion Weinstein – Words of Power the Work of Self Transformation" from Brian Scott YouTube Channel

*Sound Healing and Vibrational Awareness*
[ARTICLE] "Everything You Need to Know About Sound Healing" from MindValley website by Irina Yugay (January 10, 2019)
[ARTICLE] "What is Sound Healing?" from WellDoing website by Karen Bresloff (May 22, 2019)
[ARTICLE] "432 Hz Vs. 528 Hz: Which is Better?" from Mind Vibrations website
[ARTICLE] "440 Hz Music – The Hidden Power of Universal Vibration and Frequency" from Project:Yourself website by Ane Krstevska
[VIDEO] "Pamela Robins: The Healing Power of Sound" from LeeHarrisEnergy YouTube Channel

## APPENDIX A - Ten Ways to Enrich Your Life With Music

[ARTICLE] "Benefits of music: 5 ways to use music to improve your daily life" from UCHealth website by Kati Blocker (March 16, 2021)
[ARTICLE] "6 Profound Ways Music Improves Our Lives" from Careers in Music website by Thomas Honeyman (May 23, 2016)

## And More: BOOKS

- *Sacred Sounds: Magic & Healing Through Words & Music* by Ted Andrews
- *Tune In: A Music Therapy Approach to Life: Use Music Intentionally to Curb Stress, Boost Morale, and Restore Health* by Jennifer Buchanan
- *Feel Alive* by Ralph Smart

Book titles I have comes across (but have not read) that may be of interest:

- *The Healing Power of Sound: Recovery from Life-Threatening Illness Using Sound, Voice, and Music* by Mitchell L. Gayno
- *Music, Health and Wellbeing* by Raymond MacDonald
- *Music Medicine* by Christine Stevens
- *Your Playlist Can Change Your Life: 10 Proven Ways Your Favorite Music Can Revolutionize Your Health, Memory, Organization, Alertness and More* by Joseph Cardill

## ABOUT THE AUTHOR

John Henry Sheridan is a singer-songwriter, guitarist, teacher, composer, and musician. Along with formal musical training in both classical and jazz music, he also has accumulated several years of practical experience as a member and contributing songwriter for several groups in various genres.

His unique blend of rock, acoustic, and folk music can be found on all major music streaming platforms. John Henry's music is continually evolving. While once his music was quite heavy and serious, it now regularly incorporates more light-hearted, energetic, and kid-friendly elements.

Among his diverse teaching experiences, his work with the non-profit organization Rock Asylum showcases inter-generational teamwork through the culmination of their educational song and video "American Revolution" (2013).

In his travels throughout the world, John Henry has had the privilege to perform on four continents. The life experience and wisdom that he has gained through his world travels are a significant part of what drives him to share his life story through music, writing and speaking.

John Henry has published 3 books for beginner guitarists which implement his Single String TAB Method: *Single String Songs Vol.1, Single String Halloween Songs, Single String Exercise-Songs – Curious Creatures.* These materials have begun to be taught and learned throughout the USA as well as abroad.

Informed by his practice of Nichiren Buddhism as a member of the lay Buddhist organization SGI, he seeks to bridge people together through dialogue and the arts with the aim of co-creating a mutually supportive environment for people to flourish in a peaceful world. One manifestation of this is his livestream talk show *Music, Philosophy & More Podcast* which is a dialogue show featuring diverse people aimed at celebrating our common humanity and the beauty of each human being's journey.

His interests lie in empowering people to follow their dreams, listen to their heart, and enjoy their lives. His journeys have taken him to live abroad in Brazil and Japan. He now resides in his hometown of Marine Park, Brooklyn, NY with his family.

www.JohnHenrySheridanMusic.com
www.YouTube.com/JohnHenrySheridan

Made in United States
North Haven, CT
22 December 2021